# WORD POWER IN 21 DAYS!

## The Ultimate Challenge for Word Lovers!

J. G. Barton

# WORD REFERENCE LIBRARY

# WORD REFERENCE LIBRARY

The beauty of the English language has been fascinating to word lovers for centuries. Words define and expand our thoughts, give them new dimensions and possibilities, and ultimately, are part of the very fabric of our lives.

Word Reference Library is proud to present this book, the first in our word-lover series, for your pleasure.

*To Anne-Louise and Jeremy*

Originally published in England as 'Test Your Word Power,' and 'Boost Your Vocabulary'
©Elliot Right Way Books MCMLXXI
©Elliot Right Way Books MCMXCI
All Rights Reserved
Scrabble® is a registered trademark of the Milton Bradley Company ©1990

Book & Cover Design, Publisher Introduction, How to Use the Book, ©1993 by Word Reference Library - All Rights Reserved.
ISBN: 0-940685-35-3
Library of Congress Catalogue Card Number: 92-60916

The Author and Publisher wish to acknowledge with gratitude, some use made of the Shorter Oxford English Dictionary, third edition, by kind permission of The Clarendon Press, Oxford.

Word Reference Library books are published by Cardoza Publishing. If you are a word lover and wish to be on our mailing list, you may write to the address below.

## WORD REFERENCE LIBRARY
### Cardoza Publishing
P.O. Box 1500, Cooper Station, New York, NY 11235
(718)743-5229

# Table of Contents

## **Week Three**

### **Day Fifteen**         **112**

### **Day Sixteen**         **116**

### **Day Seventeen**         **120**

### **Day Eighteen**         **124**

### **Day Nineteen**         **129**

# How to Use This Book

Though we set up the book as a 21 day program, you may prefer to go at your own speed, perhaps one quiz a day, a pace that will give you close to three months of power learning! You may even prefer to move faster than the program.

Many of the words and quizzes we've included here are quite challenging, so the key to maximum learning is to go at your own speed, at a pace you're comfortable with.

Some words you may know, many however, will be new to you. But don't get discouraged if the tests seem difficult - the focus of this book is to teach you new words in a fun and challenging manner, not to rehash words you already may know. If the tests seem difficult, that's good. It means you're developing new word muscle.

Follow these three recommended steps to rapidly improve your vocabulary.

**Step One** - Take the daily tests (or test if you're doing a one-a- day program) and mark down your answers.

**Step Two** - Check your test results in the answer section.

**Step Three** - On the following day, after challenging the new tests, retake the previous day's tests again.

After 21 days you'll find that your vocabulary has increased dramatically.

For maximum results, keep the challenge alive and redo the program. There's a wealth of words here, too many to learn all in one shot, so this book will provide countless months of pleasure and learning as you bring your vocabulary to new and more powerful levels!

# Publisher's Introduction

Improve your word power now! Once you finish testing your skills against our 21 day power learning program, you'll notice an enormous increase in your vocabulary and have fun while learning interesting words at the same time.

We've divided the book into a fast and convenient 21 day program for word students and word lovers. Quiz by quiz and day by day, you'll notice the progressive development of a more powerful vocabulary.

Whatever your level of word skills, you'll be challenged by a collection of fascinating and useful words from all fields - manias, phobias, rare, unusual and misunderstood words, adjectives, nouns, verbs, words of shape, form and color, eponyms, homonyms, strange words and countless more!

More than a test for word lovers, this is the most comprehensive word power program ever developed. Whether you're a sophisticated logophile, writer, SAT or other test-taker, Scrabble™, word game or crossword player, this is the fastest and most fun way to immediately improve your word power!

You'll be teased, tantalized and challenged by 2,370 words - the most of any book of its kind - and in just 21 days, the fun way to learn will be paid off with a greatly increased vocabulary!

# DAY ONE

## FIND THE REAL WORDS

Some words are so odd-looking that one can hardly believe they are real words. Can you pick out the 24 real words from this list of 72 and give their meaning?

Give yourself one mark for each one identified and two extra marks if you also know its meaning.

| | |
|---|---|
| 1. Alten | 17. Melodion |
| 2. Ginglyform | 18. Residant |
| 3. Eventate | 19. Dumbrage |
| 4. Digo | 20. Gorble |
| 5. Plentitude | 21. Niddering |
| 6. Understrapper | 22. Zinky |
| 7. Brime | 23. Fusture |
| 8. Earthling | 24. Habitament |
| 9. Chapet | 25. Snig |
| 10. Dicropter | 26. Enery |
| 11. Scapple | 27. Tiesome |
| 12. Ravenish | 28. Bufflehead |
| 13. Niddling | 29. Plurry |
| 14. Absquatulate | 30. Splurge |
| 15. Middock | 31. Sidget |
| 16. Cosmoloquy | 32. Priverous |

33. Pockety

34 Midan

35. Epopt

36. Bumbelo

37. Sparilate

38. Cliable

39. Odoom

40. Snurd

41. Phluted

42. Alestered

43. Brandage

44. Rejectamenta

45. Smollish

46. Interferometer

47. Emolve

48. Snit

49. Woof

50. Weemster

51. Grunge

52. Whelving

53. Thistly

54. Ha-ha

55. Drocket

56. Superglies

57. Drabble

58. Stinwall

59. Prurn

60. Samekin

61. Quackle

62. Purgeon

63. Fenks

64. Neegle

65. Inclaim

66. Absernation

67. Abfer

68. Eoan

69. Plimwheel

70. Cogelly

71. Flart

72. Subnumate

## ANIMAL WORDS • 1

Canine is the adjective relating to dogs, from *canis*, the Latin word for dog. To which animals do these words refer?

1. Aquiline
2. Bovine
3. Ursine
4. Feline
5. Porcine
6. Leonine
7. Equine
8. Ovine
9. Asinine
10. Vulpine
11. Lupine
12. Soricine
13. Cervine
14. Leporine
15. Sciurine
16. Elephantine
17. Saurian
18. Piscine
19. Avian
20. Simian
21. Murine
22. Vespine
23. Hircine
24. Hirudinal

## ANIMAL WORDS • 2

A group or collection of cattle is known as a *herd*. What is the word for a group of these animals?

1. Squirrels
2. Lions
3. Foxes
4. Nightingales
5. Bees
6. Crows
7. Elephants
8. Eagles
9. Ravens
10. Frogs
11. Starlings
12. Rooks
13. Hounds
14. Larks
15. Gulls
16. Storks
17. Racehorses
18. Kangaroos
19. Grouse
20. Chickens
21. Geese (on water)
22. Leopards
23. Rhinoceroses
24. Porpoises

## TEST YOUR VOCABULARY • A-B
Define the following words:

1. Abyss
2. Acme
3. Acrimony
4. Aerobe
5. Affray
6. Akimbo
7. Alfresco
8. Alidade
9. Allergy
10. Amalgam
11. Amnesia
12. Amorphous
13. Anathema
14. Anodyne
15. Antediluvian
16. Aperient
17. Aplomb
18. Apophthegm
19. Arenaceous
20. Astrolabe
21. Auger
22. Augury
23. Avuncular
24. Axial
25. Bacciform
26. Bakelite
27. Barbican
28. Baroque
29. Beatification
30. Bedraggled
31. Bellicose
32. Berserk
33. Bibliophile
34. Bicentennial
35. Biograph
36. Bipartite

# DAY TWO

## ODD WORD OUT • 1

In each of the following groups all the words except one have approximately the same meaning. Which is the odd word out in each group and what is its meaning?

1. Languor, quiescence, lassitude, lethargy
2. Phlegmatic, stolid, stupid, sluggish
3. Dolorous, dismal, mournful, unmusical
4. Obstinate, assiduous, diligent, persevering
5. Astringent, ruthless, severe, austere
6. Incongruous, inconvenient, incompatible, discrepant
7. Punctilious, scrupulous, consistent, conscientious
8. Protuberant, distended, tumid, demented
9. Virulent, malignant, jejune, toxic
10. Oppressive, ravenous, rapacious, voracious
11. Debonair, modish, urbane, suave
12. Mendacious, fickle, untruthful, fictitious
13. Germane, apposite, pertinent, conducive
14. Mephitic, noxious, salacious, insalubrious
15. Precocious, naughty, premature, advanced
16. Perspicuous, discriminating, lucid, explicit
17. Desultory, refractory, contumacious, recalcitrant
18. Cacophonous, discordant, indecorous, dissonant
19. Specious, convincing, plausible, ostensible
20. Insouciant, egregious, prodigious, monstrous
21. Imply, insinuate, correspond, hint
22. Incipient, inchoate, incoherent, rudimentary
23. Concurrent, co-existent, concomitant, contingent
24. Exculpate, sequestrate, exonerate, acquit

# TEST YOUR VOCABULARY • B-C

Define the following words:

37. Blatant

38. Blather

39. Bludgeon

40. Bombast

41. Brachylogy

42. Bravado

43. Breviary

44. Bric-a-brac

45. Browbeat

46. Brusque

47. Bullace

48. Burgeon

49. Cabal

50. Cacophony

51. Cajole

52. Callisthenics

53. Candor

54. Casement

55. Censer

56. Cephalic

57. Chagrin

58. Charlatan

59. Chide

60. Circumlocution

61. Clandestine

62. Clarity

63. Clientele

64. Cognizant

65. Collimate

66. Conflagration

67. Criterion

68. Crucible

69. Cryptic

70. Cupreous

71. Curtilage

72. Cygnet

## SELECT THE RIGHT WORD

Select the word in each group of four which is nearest in meaning to the given word.

1. Acumen
     courage
     intelligence
     discernment
     veracity

2. Alacrity
     bitterness
     promptitude
     lateness
     fortitude

3. Ameliorate
     lessen
     teach
     polish
     improve

4. Antipathy
     pity
     aversion
     sympathy
     contempt

5. Astringent
     severe
     acid
     biting
     soothing

6. Bane
     upset
     cause
     curse
     flower

7. Blithe
     lonely
     contented
     gay
     active

8. Cant
     slang
     wordiness
     falsehood
     insincerity

9. Caprice
     anger
     whim
     friction
     chance

10. Cavil
     find fault
     show off
     threaten
     embezzle

11. Compendium
    suitcase
    holdall
    summary
    dictionary

12. Concoct
    make up
    lie
    slander
    fulfil

13. Consummate
    complete
    add
    subtract
    defer

14. Convulse
    miss out
    pass over
    throw
    agitate

15. Corrugated
    rusty
    grooved
    corroded
    bent

16. Coy
    backward
    naive
    bashful
    imperfect

17. Diatribe
    lecture
    sect
    reason
    invective

18. Diffuse
    dispersed
    distorted
    obscure
    clear

19. Elan
    precision
    dash
    smoothness
    virility

20. Equivocal
    equal
    horse-like
    ambiguous
    ambitious

21. Euphory
    well-being
    praise
    esteem
    gaiety

22. Flamboyant
    brash
    active
    overbearing
    florid

23. Grisly
    bear-like
    fatty
    ghastly
    whining

24. Heretical
    spiral
    unorthodox
    sealed
    old

25. Hypothesis
    assumption
    reverse
    opposite
    zenith

26. Lacerate
    upset
    divide
    tear
    inconvenience

27. Languor
    suavity
    ease
    lassitude
    rest

28. Lank
    lean
    damp
    uneven
    thick

29. Libidinous
    extravagant
    thrifty
    illiterate
    lustful

30. Lineament
    ointment
    feature
    medicine
    pedigree

31. Malevolent
    evil
    irate
    mistaken
    ill-mannered

32. Manifest
    grievous
    loud
    evident
    handy

33. Maudlin
    pitiful
    sentimental
    ringing
    melancholy

34. Mensuration
    judgement
    measurement
    incivility
    pain

35. Misanthrope
    miser
    melancholic
    witch
    man-hater

36. Miscreant
    wanderer
    spendthrift
    minister
    villain

37. Modicum
    little
    mean
    middling
    medium

38. Mullion
    mineral
    servant
    window-bar
    treasure

39. Pallid
    distressed
    pale
    poor
    superficial

40. Panacea
    remedy
    plant
    blight
    disease

41. Pathetic
    evoking pity
    incompetent
    poor
    medicinal

42. Pedagogy
    act of walking
    chiropody
    logic
    instruction

43. Peregrination
    bird-watching
    divination
    journey
    cookery

44. Pertinent
    rude
    relevant
    precise
    tidy

45. Plebeian
    banal
    flighty
    socialistic
    lower-class

46. Plenary
    absolute
    penal
    plentiful
    mean

47. Plethora
    swelling
    dogma
    excess
    profit

48. Polemic
    poisonous
    libellous
    devious
    controversial

49. Pretext
    excuse
    design
    prologue
    skill

50. Prim
    neat
    prudish
    naive
    upright

51. Raillery
    slander
    ridicule
    illegal act
    oration

52. Ratify
    excuse
    reason
    confirm
    regard

53. Regale
    entertain
    conflict
    pass over
    lose

54. Riparian
    wild
    carnivorous
    pertaining to
        river-banks
    primitive

55. Rue
    pity
    look over
    die
    regret

56. Sanctimony
    gratefulness
    assumed piety
    greed
    refuge

57. Sarcastic
    cutting
    uneven
    bad-tempered
    evil

58. Sidereal
    crippled
    sedentary
    everlasting
    relating to the
        stars

59. Sinecure
    priest
    office without
        duties
    type of chair
    medicine

60. Sophisticated
    clever
    bright
    logical
    worldy-wise

61. Spasmodic
    intermittent
    illegible
    diseased
    shoddy

62. Staid
    upright
    sedate
    retired
    unbroken

63. Stertorous
    ponderous
    questionable
    loud
    snoring heavily

64. Stigma
    reputation
    promise
    mark of
        disgrace
    part of a flower

65. Stultify
    render useless
    stifle
    stunt
    speak out

66. Succinct
    concise
    sarcastic
    sudden
    early

67. Succulent
    growing
    juicy
    young
    empty

68. Supercilious
    inconsequent
    intangible
    witty
    haughtily
       superior

69. Tarnish
    paint
    improve
    stain
    destroy

70. Tenebrous
    slender
    gloomy
    tenacious
    genuine

71. Termagant
    lizard
    sea-bird
    legal officer
    quarrelsome
       woman

72. Turpitude
    depravity
    laziness
    dirtiness
    greed

# DAY THREE

## SINGULAR WORDS

What is the plural of each of these words?

1. Thief
2. Dwarf
3. City
4. Chimney
5. Folio
6. Analysis
7. Hero
8. Larva
9. Seraph
10. Bison
11. Self
12. Roof
13. Cargo
14. Focus
15. Radius
16. Handful
17. Man-servant
18. Brother-in-law
19. Ignoramus
20. Tomato
21. Court martial
22. Index
23. Axis
24. Sphinx
25. Nebula
26. Crisis
27. Phenomenon
28. Nucleus
29. Cherub
30. Chrysalis
31. Stratum
32. Octopus
33. Graffito
34. Formula
35. Bureau
36. Stimulus

## PLURAL WORDS

What is the singular of each of these words?

1. Bacteria
2. Agenda
3. Moose
4. Lice
5. Data
6. Alumni
7. Series
8. Genera

## COMPLETE THE WORD CHALLENGE • A

Complete the following words from the given meanings.

1. A _ _ c _ _  a counting-frame with balls on wires

2. A _ t _ _ c _ t _  to dispute or wrangle

3. A _ _ m _ n _ _ l _  detestable, very unpleasant

4. Ap _ _ l _ _ n  point farthest from the sun in a planet's orbit

5. A _ g _ _ t _ _ _  like silver

6. A _ m _ n _ _ h  to warn, remind, inform or reprove

7. A _ _ m _ _ v _ _ t  to criticize or censure

8. A _ s _ _ _ h  a liqueur made from wormwood

9. A _ h _ _ m _ _ _ c  free from colour

10. As _ _ v _ _ _ t _  to solemnly declare, to assert

11. A _ _ m _ _ t  stubborn, resolute

12. A _ t _ f _ _ _  a product of human work or art

13. A _ _ r _ b _ t _  to assign or ascribe to

14. A _ _ m _ r _ t _  to outline, indicate, foreshadow

15. A _ q _ _ _ s _ _  to agree or accept

16. A _ t _ _ _ c _ _ e  a type of coal

17. An _ _ _ r _ _ _  a hermit

18. A _ r _ _ _ y  to waste away

19. A _ _ _ m _ n  animal substance, found in the white of eggs

20. A _ t _ _ m _ _ _ _ m  a defect in the focus of the eye

21. A _ r _ f _ _ _ u _  yielding gold

22. Am _ _ u _ n _ _ s  one who writes from dictation

23. A _ _ th _ _ s _ _  canonization, deification

24. A _ l _ t _ _ _ t _ _ n  words in close proximity with the same first letter

## COMPLETE THE WORD CHALLENGE • B

Complete the following words from the given meanings.

1. B _ _ v _ _ _ shortness, conciseness
2. B _ _ nd _ _ _ m _ _ t a flattering or coaxing speech or action
3. B _ st _ _ d _ _ a spectator
4. B _ _ r _ _ _ d _ a West Indian fish
5. B _ _ _ _ _ t a bunch of flowers
6. B _ v _ _ ag _ a drink
7. B _ _ c _ _ l _ a type of vegetable
8. B _ _ l _ _ _ u _ an imitation, caricature, parody
9. B _ _ z _ _ a shield, coat of arms
10. B _ t _ m _ _ mineral pitch, asphalt
11. B _ c _ _ _ _ t a card game
12. B _ _ b _ _ _ whale fat
13. B _ _ w _ r _ a rampart or defence
14. B _ g _ _ _ l _ _ a short piece of music, also a game
15. B _ _ r _ _ _ _ s _ _ the middle-class
16. B _ f _ _ c _ _ _ to branch into two, to fork
17. B _ _ f _ _ n a comic or jester
18. Br _ _ _ _ _ m a type of carriage
19. B _ z _ _ r _ grotesque, fantastic
20. B _ q _ _ _ t _ to leave by will
21. B _ m _ _ _ z _ _ to mystify or cheat somebody
22. B _ _ g _ _ _ _ n _ a two-masted vessel
23. Br _ _ d _ _ _ to wave about, flourish
24. B _ _ st _ _ _ _ s rough, noisy

## VERBS • 1

The precise use of verbs is essential to good English. Define the following verbs.

| | |
|---|---|
| 1. Amputate | 19. Revivify |
| 2. Bicker | 20. Scrimp |
| 3. Cashier | 21. Strangulate |
| 4. Conjecture | 22. Transgress |
| 5. Delineate | 23. Vivisect |
| 6. Emulate | 24. Whet |
| 7. Fluctuate | 25. Adjudicate |
| 8. Gerrymander | 26. Bombard |
| 9. Hamstring | 27. Confiscate |
| 10. Hector | 28. Controvert |
| 11. Incite | 29. Devastate |
| 12. Legislate | 30. Emasculate |
| 13. Meander | 31. Flounder |
| 14. Militate | 32. Glisten |
| 15. Nonplus | 33. Hoax |
| 16. Objurgate | 34. Indemnify |
| 17. Percolate | 35. Inculcate |
| 18. Prorogue | 36. Liquefy |

# DAY FOUR

## SHAPES

What shape or form does each word signify?

1. Floriform
2. Dendriform
3. Unciform
4. Cuneiform
5. Campaniform
6. Luniform
7. Fusiform
8. Calciform
9. Flabelliform
10. Cribriform
11. Linguiform
12. Nasiform
13. Hastiform
14. Napiform
15. Aliform
16. Reniform
17. Penniform
18. Scutiform
19. Cruciform
20. Vermiform
21. Tympaniform
22. Conchiform
23. Nubiform
24. Auriform

## COLORS

What color would describe each of these colors and pigments?

1. Burnt sienna
2. Ochre
3. Russet
4. Azure
5. Crimson
6. Carmine
7. Titian
8. Sepia
9. Magenta
10. Vermilion
11. Amber
12. Maroon
13. Scarlet
14. Gamboge
15. Auburn
16. Veridian

## COMPLETE THE WORD CHALLENGE • C

Complete the following words from the given meanings.

1. C _ _ l _ p _ _ n _ a transparent wrapping material
2. C _ _ y _ _ r _ an old Scottish sword
3. C _ _ v _ _ _ _ a small naval vessel
4. C _ n _ c _ _ sneering, derisive
5. C _ t _ s _ _ _ p _ _ a disaster, calamity
6. C _ t _ _ _ l a fortress or castle
7. C _ _ s _ _ c _ _ _ s class of animals with hard shells
8. C _ l _ _ t _ to compare in detail
9. C _ t _ c _ _ _ s underground cemeteries or chambers
10. C _ b _ _ _ t a kind of entertainment
11. C _ p _ _ c _ _ _ s subject to whim, inconstant
12. C _ n _ _ t _ n _ t _ to link together
13. C _ _ l _ _ _ c angry, irascible
14. C _ n _ _ n _ _ s general agreement or opinion
15. C _ _ h _ _ _ t a type of whale
16. C _ _ t _ _ _ _ _ _ l tending to fly off from the center
17. C _ c _ _ _ n _ t _ to laugh loudly
18. C _ _ t _ m _ _ i _ _ _ disobedient, insubordinate
19. C _ _ ff _ _ _ _ r type of low cupboard with a top
20. C _ _ g _ l _ _ _ to solidify or clot
21. C _ r _ _ r _ _ d _ m a polishing-stone
22. C _ m _ _ _ b _ _ d a waist-sash
23. Cr _ _ _ l _ _ _ _ d furnished with battlements
24. C _ _ k _ _ _ the husband of an unfaithful wife

## TEST YOUR VOCABULARY • D-E
Define the following words:

1. Dais

2. Dawdle

3. Debilitate

4. Debonair

5. Decrepit

6. Deflagrate

7. Demoniac

8. Denizen

9. Depilate

10. Dermatology

11. Diaphanous

12. Didactic

13. Dilatory

14. Discrepant

15. Disquisition

16. Dodecagon

17. Dolorous

18. Dragoman

19. Drollery

20. Drowsy

21. Dryad

22. Dudgeon

23. Dulcet

24. Dyne

25 Ebullient

26. Echelon

27. Eclogue

28. Educe

29. Effete

30. Effulgent

31. Egregious

32. Electrode

33. Elision

34. Emanate

35. Emolument

36. Encomium

# DAY FIVE

## MATERIALS
**With what materials are these workers associated?**

1. Currier
2. Glazier
3. Brazier
4. Fuller
5. Joiner
6. Blacksmith
7. Mercer
8. Sawyer
9. Haberdasher
10. Pharmacist
11. Assayer
12. Bibliographer

## PRODUCTS
**What is made or repaired by these workers?**

1. Cooper
2. Bowyer
3. Fletcher
4. Cordwainer
5. Cutler
6. Tinker
7. Cartographer
8. Plumber
9. Tailor
10. Cobbler
11. Chandler
12. Draughtsman

## TOOLS AND INSTRUMENTS
**Who would use these tools or instruments?**

1. Lightmeter
2. Dibble
3. Scalpel
4. Last
5. Hod
6. Stethoscope
7. Capstan
8. Clinometer
9. Anemometer
10. Piton
11. Wheelbrace
12. Palette

## TEST YOUR VOCABULARY • E-F
Define the following words:

37. Ennui

38. Ephemeral

39. Epigram

40. Epitaph

41. Epithet

42. Epitome

43. Erudite

44. Estimable

45. Eulogize

46. Evaluate

47. Evoke

48. Exegesis

49. Facile

50. Factitious

51. Faience

52. Fallible

53. Fastidious

54. Fecund

55. Ferrule

56. Fervor

57. Figurine

58. Fissile

59. Flagrant

60. Flatulent

61. Flippant

62. Flocculent

63. Foliage

64. Formulate

65. Fortuitous

66. Fractious

67. Fructify

68. Fugacious

69. Fumigate

70. Funereal

71. Furbish

72. Furor

## COMPLETE THE WORD CHALLENGE • D

Complete the following words from the given meanings.

1. D _ s _ _ _ _ l _ _  not alike
2. D _ _ _ _ _ y  a line of hereditary rulers
3. D _ _ _ s _ _ n  ridicule, mockery
4. D _ b _ _ l _  a breaking-up, rout, stampede
5. D _ _ f _ _ e _ t  lacking self-confidence, bashful
6. D _ a _ _ _ c  vigorously effective, violent
7. D _ _ r _ s  wreckage, accumulated fragments
8. Di _ _ g _ _ l _  balloon, airship
9. D _ m _ _ c _ t _  to mark or define the boundary of
10. D _ c _ _ _ _ t  in a state of decay or decline
11. D _ _ t _ r _ _ y  skill, adroitness
12. D _ l _ _ t _ _ _ e  lover of the arts, one who toys with a subject
13. D _ w _ _ _ r  a titled or propertied lady
14. D _ s _ _ l _ _ e  morally lax, licentious
15. D _ r _ g _ t _ _ _  disparaging, detracting from
16. Di _ _ ip _ _ _  to disperse, scatter, squander
17. D _ n _ g _ _ _ _  to defame, blacken the name of
18. D _ _ l _ v _ _ _  a downward slope
19. D _ m _ _ ee _  to tyrannize, be overbearing
20. Do _ i _ _ l _  home or residence
21. D _ _ h _ h _ _ g  a union of two vowels pronounced in one syllable
22. D _ _ _ _ n _  asleep, inactive
23. D _ _ _ l _ c _  abandoned
24. D _ _ _ i _ r _ _ e  tooth-powder

## NAME THE CORRECT NOUN • 1

Name the noun that fits each of these definitions.

1. A public slaughterhouse for cattle.
2. Annihilation or extermination of a race or nation.
3. Ornamental candlestick or lampstand.
4. Picture or carving formed of three hinged panels.
5. Crossbar suspended by cords as a swing for acrobats.
6. Grotesque or ludicrous representation of a person by exaggeration of characteristics.
7. Acrobat who twists and distorts the body out of shape.
8. Uncultured person with material interests.
9. Substance that aids chemical change without itself changing.
10. Mythical reptile with lethal breath and look.
11. Lace veil worn by Spanish women over head and shoulders.
12. Person who migrates to a country as a settler.
13. Raft with two or more parallel logs, or boat with twin hulls.
14. Large heavy motor vehicle named after Hindu idol.
15. Delicate tracery of gold or silver or other metal wire.
16. Apparatus like an umbrella for descending from a height.
17. Written statement for use as judicial evidence.
18. The skull, or bones enclosing the brain.
19. Food made from milk fermented by added bacteria.
20. Underground edible fungus esteemed as a delicacy.
21. Body suspended so as to swing or oscillate by gravity.
22. Beautiful handwriting or penmanship.
23. Pair of eyeglasses with a long handle.
24. Trial model, original or preliminary version of a thing.

# DAY SIX

## "-OCRACY" AND "-ARCHY"

The suffix "-cracy" comes from a Greek word meaning "power" or "rule"; an "o" was later added to form the familiar ending "-ocracy", and it was used as a nonce-word (i.e. a temporary word) to mean rule by any particular class; e.g. "aristocracy" means "rule by noblemen".

The suffix "-archy" is also derived from a Greek word meaning "to rule"; e.g. "oligarchy" means "rule by the few". Who are the rulers in the following systems?

| **"-OCRACY** | **"-ARCHY"** |
|---|---|
| 1. Autocracy | 13. Anarchy |
| 2. Bureaucracy | 14. Decadarchy |
| 3. Democracy | 15. Gynarchy |
| 4. Dulocracy | 16. Hagiarchy |
| 5. Gerontocracy | 17. Hecatontarchy |
| 6. Kakistocracy | 18. Heptarchy |
| 7. Monocracy | 19. Matriarchy |
| 8. Pantisocracy | 20. Monarchy |
| 9. Plutocracy | 21. Octarchy |
| 10. Ptochocracy | 22. Patriarchy |
| 11. Stratocracy | 23. Pentarchy |
| 12. Theocracy | 24. Triarchy |

### Who are or were the following rulers?

| | |
|---|---|
| 25. Sultan | 28. Ameer, Amir or Emir |
| 26. Nabob | 29. Doge |
| 27. Nizam | 30. Shah |

## COMPLETE THE WORD CHALLENGE • E

Complete the following words from the given meanings.

1. E _ p _ t _ a _ _ to speak or write at some length
2. E _ _ r _ _ e _ us  external, foreign
3. E _ l _ c _ _ c  borrowed from various sources, not exclusive
4. E _ _ g _ _  a riddle or puzzle
5. E _ _ n _ _ c _ _ t  quickly vanishing, fleeting
6. E _ _ c _ r _ _ t _  to embitter, aggravate, irritate
7. E _ v _ _ _ n _ _ n _  surrounding area or circumstances
8. El _ _ _ r _ t _  to work out in detail, enlarge upon
9. E _ qu _ _ _ t _  that which arouses great admiration, acute
10. E _ _ ul _ _ t _  ornamental shoulder-piece of a uniform
11. E _ f _ _ v _ _ c _  to give off gaseous bubbles
12. E _ v _ s _ _ e  to face or contemplate
13. E _ _ e _ e _ l  light, airy, spirit-like
14. E _ _ rv _ _ _  to weaken
15. E _ i _ _ e  fit to be eaten
16. E _ b _ _ z _ _  to divert money to one's own use fraudulently
17. E _ _ i _ c _  that which has died out
18. E _ _ on _ _ _ s  mistaken, incorrect
19. E _ _ l _ _ nt  flowing out
20. E _ c _ _ p _ t _  to free from blame, exonerate
21. En _ _ _ st _ _  painting by burning in
22. E _ _ l _ g _ _  a speech or poem at the end of a play
23. E _ _ _ r  a young eel
24. Ex _ _ e _ _ v _  an oath or exclamation

## TEST YOUR VOCABULARY • G-H
Define the following words:

1. Galaxy
2. Gallimaufry
3. Galore
4. Gambit
5. Garish
6. Garniture
7. Garrulous
8. Gauche
9. Genealogy
10. Genteel
11. Genuflect
12. Gibberish
13. Gingerly
14. Glaciated
15. Glandiferous
16. Gorgeous
17. Grandeur
18. Gratuitous
19. Gregarious
20. Grotto
21. Guillemot
22. Gumption
23. Gymkhana
24. Gyrate
25. Habituate
26. Haematite
27. Haggard
28. Hallucination
29. Harass
30. Hastate
31. Hedonism
32. Heinous
33. Hemlock
34. Hereditament
35. Heterogeneous
36. Hiatus

# DAY SEVEN

## NAME THE CORRECT NOUN • 2

Name the noun that fits each of these definitions.

25. A hackneyed or stereotyped phrase or expression.
26. Wall arcade or gallery in a church above the nave arcade.
27. Maze or tortuous network of passages.
28. Traitor or collaborationist named after a Norwegian.
29. Noisy mischievous ghost or spirit.
30. One who speaks or writes several laguages.
31. Thick cushion for kneeling in church.
32. Large shed for housing aircraft.
33. Plant that lives for several years.
34. Piece of land almost surrounded by water or projecting into the sea.
35. Ring-shaped coral reef enclosing a lagoon.
36. District under the pastoral care of a bishop.
37. Lower part of the human body below the diaphragm.
38. The universe as a well-ordered whole or system.
39. Place where bees and beehives are kept.
40. Plane figure with six sides and six angles.
41. Young hare, especially one in its first year.
42. Mounted man with a lance in a bullfight.
43. Tree cut back to produce close growth of young branches.
44. Person of wide learning acquainted with many subjects.
45. Meeting or social event for boat or yacht races.
46. Staff or wand borne as a symbol of authority or sovereignty.
47. Himalayan animal known as the "abominable snowman".
48. Popular newspaper with news in concentrated form.

## COMPLETE THE WORD CHALLENGE • F

Complete the following words from the given meanings.

1. F _ _ t _ t _ _ _ s  not real, counterfeit, imaginary
2. F _ r _ c _ o_ _  fierce, savage, cruel
3. F _ n _ s _ _  artfulness, delicate manipulation
4. F _ o _ _ s _ _ _ t  flowering
5. F _ _ n _ _ y  servant or footman
6. F _ _ _ c _ _ _ r  type of cable railway
7. F _ _ u _ u _  silly, idiotic
8. Fo _ _ _ d _ _ le  hard to overcome or defeat
9. F _ l _ _ f _  misrepresent, alter
10. F _ _ _ b _ _ g _ _ t _ _  dumbfounded, astonished
11. F _ _ m _ _ t  something invented or imagined
12. F _ _ _ _ g _ n _ _ _  containing iron
13. F _ u _ _ l  careful, sparing
14. F _ l _ c _ _ _ us  apt, happy in manner
15. F _ r _ b _ _ i _ _  an omen or presentiment
16. Fr _ _ _ r _ _ _ e  to associate or make friends with
17. F _ b _ _ c _ t _  to invent or "make up"
18. F _ _ s _ r _  a cleft or narrow opening
19. F _ u _ t _ _ _  enjoyment from possession or realization of something
20. F _ _ eti _ _ s  waggish, jocular
21. F _ _ t _ _ l _  a fleet of boats
22. F _ _ v _ l _ _ _  paltry, trifling, not serious
23. F _ r _ _ t _ _ e  courage in adversity
24. F _ _ x _ _ l _  pliable, supple, adaptable

## RARE WORDS • 1

Many words are seldom used in everyday language. Here are some of these uncommon words; most of them however have simpler and more straightforward meanings than many common words. If you get three or more definitions correct, give yourself a pat on the back!

1. Adipescent
2. Aduncous
3. Albescent
4. Ammophilous
5. Atimy
6. Bibacious
7. Buccinatory
8. Calcariform
9. Cataplexy
10. Cespitose
11. Chiaroscuro
12. Chironomy
13. Cicatrice
14. Clepsydra
15. Contabescent
16. Crepuscular
17. Deliquescence
18. Divarication
19. Eccaleobion
20. Edentate
21. Eleemosynary
22. Epalpebrate
23. Epistaxis
24. Fellifluous
25. Fimbriated
26. Fissiparous
27. Funiform
28. Geophagist
29. Glossologist
30. Gummous
31. Hagiolatry
32. Hecatomb
33. Homodont
34. Ianthine
35. Idiograph
36. Immiscible

# WEEK ONE ANSWERS

## - DAY ONE ANSWERS -

### Find the Real Words (page 11)
These are the real words and their meanings.

2. Ginglyform - hinge-shaped.
6. Understrapper - a subordinate, an underling.
8. Earthling - an inhabitant of the earth.
11. Scapple - to reduce the faces of a stone block to a place surface.
14. Absquatulate - to leave hurriedly, to abscond.
17. Melodion - an obsolete wind instrument, a type of accordion.
21. Niddering - a coward; base or cowardly.
22. Zinky - relating to or containing zinc.
25. Snig - a young or small eel.
28. Bufflehead - a fool, a blockhead.
30. Splurge - ostentatious display, heavy splash.
33. Pockety - said of a mine having pockets of ore.
35. Epopt - a beholder.
36. Bumbelo - a glass vessel for subliming camphor.
39. Odoom - a West African timber tree.
44. Rejectamenta - useless or worthless things, refuse.
46. Interferometer - instrument for measuring lengths by rays of light.
49. Woof - woven fabric or thread.
53. Thistly - like a thistle, full of thistles.
54. Ha-ha - a sunken fence or boundary.
57. Drabble - to become wet and dirty, to fish with rod and line.
61. Quackle - to quack like a duck.
63. Fenks - the parts of the whale blubber which contain oil.
68. Eoan - pertaining to the dawn, eastern.

## Animal Words • 1 (page 13)

| | | |
|---|---|---|
| 1. Eagles | 9. Asses | 17. Lizards |
| 2. Oxen | 10. Foxes | 18. Fish |
| 3. Bears | 11. Wolves | 19. Birds |
| 4. Cats | 12. Shrew-mice | 20. Apes |
| 5. Swine | 13. Deer | 21. Mice |
| 6. Lions | 14. Hares | 22. Wasps |
| 7. Horses | 15. Squirrels | 23. Goats |
| 8. Sheep | 16. Elephants | 24. Leeches |

## Animal Words • 2 (page 13 )

| | | |
|---|---|---|
| 1. Dray | 9. Unkindness | 17. String |
| 2. Pride, flock or troop | 10. Army | 18. Troop |
| 3. Skulk or earth | 11. Chattering | 19. Covey or pack |
| 4. Watch | 12. Clamor | 20. Brood |
| 5. Swarm | 13. Pack | 21. Gaggle |
| 6. Murder | 14. Exaltation | 22. Leap |
| 7. Herd | 15. Colony | 23. Crash |
| 8. Convocation | 16. Mustering | 24. School |

## Test Your Vocabulary • 1 (page 17)

1. a bottomless chasm, deep gorge, bowels of the earth
2. the highest point or pitch, the culmination or perfection
3. bitterness of temper or manner
4. a microbe living on free oxygen from the air
5. a breach of the peace, caused by fighting in a public place
6. hand on hip and elbow turned outward
7. in the open air
8. a surveying instrument, or part of one, which measures vertical angles
9. sensitiveness to certain foods, insect bites, etc.
10. mixture of metal with mercury, mixture of any two substances

11. loss of memory
12. shapeless, formless
13. an accursed thing, curse of the Church, an imprecation
14. medicine or drug which alleviates pain, anything soothing
15. relating or referring to the period before the Flood
16. laxative
17. confidence, self-possession, perpendicularity
18. a terse, pointed saying, a pithy maxim
19. sandy, sand-like (referring to soils)
20. an instrument formerly used for taking altitudes
21. a tool for boring holes in wood or in the earth
22. an omen, portent, presentiment
23. of or like an uncle
24. round an axis, forming an axis
25. berry-shaped
26. a synthetic resin or plastic
27. an outer defence to a city or castle
28. grotesque, odd (especially of a style of architecture)
29. the action of making, or being made, blessed
30. hanging or trailing limply wet
31. inclined to war, warlike
32. a state of frenzied fury
33. a lover of books
34. occurring every two hundred years, lasting two hundred years
35. an early form of cinematograph
36. divided into two parts, drawn up in two parts

## - DAY TWO ANSWERS -

### Odd Word Out • 1 (page 16)

1. Quiescence- quietness, immobility
2. Stupid - slow-witted, dull, obtuse
3. Unmusical - not musical, inharmonious
4. Obstinate - stubborn, inflexible
5. Ruthless - without pity or compassion
6. Inconvenient - awkward, troublesome, unsuitable
7. Consistent - compatible, not contradictory
8. Demented - crazed, insane
9. Jejune - unsatisfying, dull, insipid
10. Oppressive - overpowering, overwhelming
11. Modish - fashionable
12. Fickle - inconstant, changeable
13. Conducive - leading to or contributing to
14. Salacious -lustful, lecherous
15. Naughty - disobedient, ill-behaved
16. Discriminating - making a distinction, differentiating
17. Desultory - unmethodical, skipping about, random
18. Indecorous - in bad taste, improper
19. Convincing - persuasive, carrying conviction
20. Insouciant - careless, indifferent, unconcerned
21. Correspond - be in harmony, similar to, communicate
22. Incoherent - not connected, disjointed
23. Contingent - incidental to, conditional, accidental
24. Sequestrate - appropriate, confiscate, seize possession of

### Test Your Vocabulary • B-C  (page 17)

37. noisy, clamorous, offensively loud
38. loquacious nonsense
39. a short stick or club used as a weapon, to strike with one

40. inflated, turgid or empty language
41. condensed expression, over-conciseness of speech
42. boastful behaviour or show of courage
43. a brief statement, the book containing the "Divine Office"
44. old curiosities, antiquarian odds-and-ends
45. to bully, bear down with words or looks
46. blunt, offhand (of mannner or speech)
47. wild plum tree, wild plum
48. to put forth buds, to sprout, a young bud
49. a private intrigue, secret meeting, clique
50. an ill sound or discord
51. to persuade by flattery, specious promises, deceit etc.
52. exercises for developing the figure
53. frankness, ingenuousness
54. type of window-frame
55. a vessel in which incense is burnt
56. of or relating to the head
57. mortification arising from disappointment or failure
58. an impostor, quack, pretender to knowledge
59. to scold, rebuke
60. the use of many words instead of few, a roundabout expression
61. secret, concealed, underhand, surreptitious
62. clearness
63. a body of clients, supporters or customers, a following
64. having knowledge of, being aware of
65. to adjust line of sight (of telescopes), make parallel
66. a large, destructive fire
67. a principle or standard by which something is judged
68. a vessel made to endure great heat, a severe trial
69. secret, occult, mystical
70. of or containing copper, copper-colored
71. an area attached to a house, forming one enclosure with it
72. a young swan

## Select The Right Word (page 18)

1. discernment
2. promptitude
3. improve
4. aversion
5. severe
6. curse
7. gay
8. insincerity
9. whim
10. find fault
11. summary
12. make up
13. complete
14. agitate
15. grooved
16. bashful
17. invective
18. dispersed
19. dash
20. ambiguous
21. well-being
22. florid
23. ghastly
24. unorthodox
25. assumption
26. tear
27. lassitude
28. lean
29. lustful
30. feature
31. evil
32. evident
33. sentimental
34. measurement
35. man-hater
36. villain
37. little
38. window-bar
39. pale
40. remedy
41. evoking pity
42. instruction
43. journey
44. relevant
45. lower-class
46. absolute
47. excess
48. controversial
49. excuse
50. prudish
51. ridicule
52. confirm
53. entertain
54. pertaining to river-banks
55. regret
56. assumed piety
57. cutting
58. relating to the stars
59. office without duties
60. worldly-wise
61. intermittent
62. sedate
63. snoring heavily
64. mark of disgrace
65. render useless
66. concise
67. juicy
68. haughtily superior
69. stain
70. gloomy
71. quarrelsome woman
72. depravity

## - DAY THREE ANSWERS -

### Singular Words (page 26)

1. Thieves
2. Dwarfs
3. Cities
4. Chimneys
5. Folios
6. Analyses
7. Heroes
8. Larvae
9. Seraphs or seraphim
10. Bison
11. Selves
12. Roofs
13. Cargoes
14. Foci or focuses
15. Radii
16. Handfuls
17. Men-servants
18. Brothers-in-law
19. Ignoramuses
20. Tomatoes
21. Courts martial
22. Indexes or indices
23. Axes
24. Sphinxes or sphinges
25. Nebulae
26. Crises
27. Phenomena
28. Nuclei or nucleuses
29. Cherubs or cherubim
30. Chrysalises or chrysalides
31. Strata
32. Octopuses or octopodes
33. Graffiti
34. Formulae or formulas
35. Bureaus or bureaux
36. Stimuli

### Plural Words (page 26)

1. Bacterium
2. Agendum
3. Moose
4. Louse
5. Datum
6. Alumnus
7. Series
8. Genus

### Complete the Word Challenge • A (page 27)

1. Abacus
2. Alercate
3. Abominable
4. Aphelion
5. Argentine
6. Admonish
7. Animadvert
8. Absinth
9. Achromatic
10. Asseverate
11. Adamant
12. Artefact
13. Attribute
14. Adumbrate
15. Acquiesce
16. Anthracite
17. Anchorite
18. Atrophy
19. Albumen
20. Astigmatism
21. Auriferous
22. Amanuensis
23. Apotheosis
24. Alliteration

### Complete the Word Challenge • B (page 28)

1. Brevity
2. Blandishment
3. Bystander
4. Barracuda
5. Bouquet
6. Beverage
7. Broccoli
8. Burlesque
9. Blazon
10. Bitumen
11. Baccarat
12. Blubber
13. Bulwark
14. Bagatelle
15. Bourgeoisie
16. Bifurcate
17. Buffoon
18. Brougham
19. Bizarre
20. Bequeath
21. Bamboozle
22. Brigantine
23. Brandish
24. Boisterous

### Verbs • 1 (page 29)

1. cut off a limb or any projecting part of the body
2. quarrel, wrangle, fight
3. dismiss from position of command or authority, depose
4. form an opinion on insufficient grounds, guess, surmise
5. outline, sktech out, portray
6. strive to equal or rival, vie with
7. vary, vacillate, waver, undergo changes
8. manipulate in order to gain unfair advantage (especially in elections)
9. cripple, destroy efficiency of
10. brag, bluster, domineer, bully
11. urge or spur on, stimulate
12. make or enact laws
13. wind about, wander deviously or aimlessly
14. tell against a conclusion or result
15. perplex, bring to a standstill, render ineffective
16. chide, scold
17. strain, filter, permeate or trickle through
18. discontinue meetings, dismiss by authority
19. revive, reinvigorate, put new life into
20. economize, cut short, be niggardly

21. choke, stifle, suffocate
22. break, violate, infringe, trespass against
23. dissect while living
24. sharpen, render acute or eager
25. determine judicially, act as judge
26. batter with shot and shell
27. seize as if by authority, appropriate
28. dispute, deny, oppose in argument
29. lay waste, ravage, render desolate
30. weaken, enfeeble, deprive of strength
31. struggle clumsily, plunge, roll and tumble about
32. glitter, sparkle, shine with twinkling light
33. deceive, play upon credulity of
34. secure against loss, compensate for
35. teach forcibly, impress by repetition
36. reduce to liquid, become liquid

## - DAY FOUR ANSWERS -

### Shapes (page31)

| | | |
|---|---|---|
| 1. Flower | 9. Fan | 17. Feather |
| 2. Tree | 10. Sieve | 18. Shield |
| 3. Hook | 11. Tongue | 19. Cross |
| 4. Wedge | 12. Nose | 20. Worm |
| 5. Bell | 13. Spear | 21. Drum |
| 6. Moon | 14. Turnip | 22. Shell |
| 7. Spindle | 15. Wing | 23. Cloud |
| 8. Pebble | 16. Kidney | 24. Ear |

### Colors (page 31)

1. Reddish-brown
2. Brownish-yellow
3. Reddish-brown
4. Blue
5. Deep red
6. Red/crimson
7. Red
8. Brown
9. Brilliant crimson
10. Red/scarlet
11. Yellow
12. Brownish-crimson
13. Bright red
14. Yellow
15. Reddish-brown
16. Green

### Complete the Word Challenge • C (page 32)

1. Cellophane
2. Claymore
3. Corvette
4. Cynical
5. Catastrophe
6. Citadel
7. Crustaceans
8. Collate
9. Catacombs
10. Cabaret
11. Capricious
12. Concatenate
13. Choleric
14. Consensus
15. Cachalot
16. Centrifugal
17. Cachinnate
18. Contumacious
19. Chiffonier
20. Coagulate
21. Carborundum
22. Cummerbund
23. Crenellated
24. Cuckold

### Test Your Vocabulary • D-E (page 33)

1. a raised platform
2. to idle, loiter, waste time
3. to enfeeble, make weak
4. genial, pleasant, affable
5. worn out with age, old and feeble
6. to cause to burn away rapidly, to burst into flame and burn rapidly
7. devilish, like a demon, possessed by an evil spirit
8. an inhabitant or occupant, a foreigner admitted to residence
9. to remove the hair from
10. the science of the skin and its diseases

11. permitting light to pass through, transparent
12. having the manner of a teacher, instructive
13. tending to cause or designed to cause delay, given to delay
14. dissimilar, discordant, inconsistent
15. a lengthy treatise or discourse on a subject
16. a plane figure of twelve sides and angles
17. dismal, doleful, distressing
18. an interpreter or guide in the Middle East
19. quaint humor, jesting
20. sleepy, sluggish, soporific
21. a tree- or wood-nymph
22. a feeling of anger, resentment or offence
23. sweet to the ear, pleasing, soothing
24. a unit of force
25. boiling, exuberant, bubbling over
26. formation of troops etc., in which divisions are parallel but staggered
27. a short poem, especially a pastoral dialogue
28. to bring out, develop, give rise to
29. exhausted, worn out, incapable
30. shining brilliantly, radiant
31. remarkable, gross, shocking, flagrant
32. either pole of an electric battery
33. the dropping or suppression of a vowel or syllable in or between words
34. to flow forth, issue from, originate
35. profit or salary from office or employment
36. formal or high-flown praise

## - DAY FIVE ANSWERS -

### Materials (page 35)

1. leather
2. glass
3. brass
4. cloth
5. wood
6. iron
7. textile fabrics
8. timber
9. thread, ribbons, etc.
10. drugs and medicine
11. metals
12. books

### Products (page 35)

1. casks and barrels
2. bows
3. arrows
4. shoes
5. knives etc.
6. pots and pans
7. maps
8. pipes
9. clothes
10. boots and shoes
11. candles
12. plans, sketches and drawings

### Tools and Instruments (page 35)

1. photographer
2. gardener
3. surgeon
4. shoemaker
5. bricklayer
6. doctor
7. sailor
8. surveyor
9. meteorologist
10. mountaineer
11. automobile mechanic
12. painter

### Test Your Vocabulary • E-F (page 36)

37. mental weariness from want of occupation or interest
38. short-lived, transitory, lasting only a day or so
39. a short poem with witty ending, a pointed saying
40. an inscription on a tomb
41. an adjective expressing quality or attribute of person or thing
42. a summary, abstract, record in miniature

43. learned, scholarly
44. worthy of esteem or regard
45. to commend, extol, praise
46. to find the amount of, work out the value of
47. to call forth, summon up (spirits, etc.)
48. an explanation, exposition
49. easily done, working easily, fluent, gentle
50. unnatural, artificial
51. kinds of glazed earthenware and porcelain
52. liable to be deceived or to err, liable to be in error
53. easily disgusted, squeamish
54. fruitful, prolific, fertile
55. a metal ring or cap which strengthens end of a stick, etc.
56. glowing, intense heat, passion, vehemence, zeal
57. a small carved or sculptured figure
58. inclined to split, capable of being split
59. glaring, scandalous
60. generating gas in the stomach, puffed-up, pretentious
61. showing unwanted levity, lacking in gravity or respect
62. like tufts of wool, woolly
63. leaves, leafage
64. to reduce to or express in a formula, set forth systematically
65. accidental, casual, produced by chance
66. refractory, unruly, cross
67. to bear fruit, become fruitful
68. fleeting, evanescent, fugitive
69. to disinfect or purify by means of smoke or fumes, to perfume
70. relating to a funeral, dismal, melancholy, mournful
71. polish up, burnish, renovate, revive
72. a rage, craze or enthusiastic admiration

## Complete the Word Challenge • D (page 37)

1. Dissimilar
2. Dynasty
3. Derision
4. Debacle
5. Diffident
6. Drastic
7. Debris
8. Dirigible
9. Demarcate
10. Decadent
11. Dexterity
12. Dilettante
13. Dowager
14. Dissolute
15. Derogatory
16. Dissipate
17. Denigrate
18. Declivity
19. Domineer
20. Domicile
21. Diphthong
22. Dormant
23. Derelict
24. Dentifrice

## Name the Correct Word • 1 (page 38)

1. Abattoir
2. Genocide
3. Candelabrum
4. Triptych
5. Trapeze
6. Caricature
7. Contortionist
8. Philistine
9. Catalyst
10. Basilisk
11. Mantilla
12. Immigrant
13. Catamaran
14. Juggernaut
15. Filigree
16. Parachute
17. Affidavit
18. Cranium
19. Yoghurt
20. Truffle
21. Pendulum
22. Calligraphy
23. Lorgnette
24. Prototype

## - DAY SIX ANSWERS -

### "-Ocracy" and "-Archy" (page 40)

1. Rule by: absolute authority, a ruler with absolute power
2. officials
3. the people
4. slaves
5. old men
6. the worst citizens
7. one person
8. everybody (all are equal)
9. the rich
10. the poor
11. the military
12. a deity or God
13. nobody - it means an absence of government
14. ten persons
15. a woman or women
16. priests or saints
17. a hundred persons
18. seven persons
19. the mother as the head of the family
20. a king or queen
21. eight persons
22. the father or founder, or head of a Church
23. five persons
24. three persons
25. sovereign of a Mohammedan country, especially Turkey
26. governor of an Indian district
27. herditary ruler of Hyderabad
28. Mohammedan ruler of Sind and Afghanistan
29. chief magistrate in the Republics of Venice and Genoa
30. King of Persia

### Complete the Word Challenge • E (page 41)

1. Expatiate
2. Extraneous
3. Eclectic
4. Enigma
5. Evanescent
6. Exacerbate
7. Environment
8. Elaborate
9. Exquisite
10. Epaulette
11. Effervesce
12. Envisage
13. Ethereal
14. Enervate
15. Edible
16. Embezzle
17. Extinct
18. Erroneous
19. Effluent
20. Exculpate
21. Encaustic
22. Epilogue
23. Elver
24. Expletive

### Test Your Vocabulary • G-H (page 42)

1. a luminous band of stars, a crowd of distinguished people
2. a mixture, jumble , medley
3. in plenty or abundance
4. an opening move, especially in a game of chess
5. obtrusively or excessively bright, showy, gaudy
6. appurtenances, adornment, trimming, dressing
7. loquacious, wordy
8. awkward, clumsy
9. the study of pedigrees, tracing of person's ancestors
10. well-dressed, elegant, characteristics of upper classes
11. to kneel or bend the knee
12. unintelligible speech, jargon
13. cautiously, timidly
14. marked, polished or eroded by ice action, covered by glaciers
15. bearing acorns or similar fruit
16. richly coloured, magnificent, showy, dazzling
17. great power, majesty, splendour of living
18. freely given or obtained, uncalled for, unjustifiable
19. living in flocks or communities, fond of company
20. a picturesque cave or cavern, often artificial
21. a species of sea-birds
22. common sense, shrewdness, resource, a vehicle for color (painting)
23. an athletic-sports display, a place for such a display
24. to move in a circle, revolve, whirl
25. to fix in a habit, to accustom to
26. an iron ore
27. (of a person) wild-looking, gaunt: (of a hawk) wild, untamed
28. an illusion, the perception of an object not actually present
29. to vex, trouble, worry, wear out or exhaust
30. spear-shaped
31. the doctrine that pleasure is the chief good

32. infamous, atrocious, highly criminal
33. a poisonous plant
34. property that can be inherited, real property, inheritance
35. diverse in character, of diverse elements
36. a break or gap in a series or chain, or between two vowels

## - DAY SEVEN -

### Name the Correct Word • 2 (page 44)

| | | |
|---|---|---|
| 25. Cliche | 33. Perennial | 41. Leveret |
| 26. Triforium | 34. Peninsula | 42. Picador |
| 27. Labyrinth | 35. Atoll | 43. Pollard |
| 28. Quisling | 36. Diocese | 44. Polymath |
| 29. Poltergeist | 37. Abdomen | 45. Regatta |
| 30. Polyglot | 38. Cosmos | 46. Sceptre |
| 31. Hassock | 39. Apiary | 47. Yeti |
| 32. Hangar | 40. Hexagon | 48. Tabloid |

### Complete the Word Challenge • F (page 45)

| | | |
|---|---|---|
| 1. Fictitious | 9. Falsify | 17. Fabricate |
| 2. Ferocious | 10. Flabbergasted | 18. Fissure |
| 3. Finesse | 11. Figment | 19. Fruition |
| 4. Florescent | 12. Ferruginous | 20. Facetious |
| 5. Flunkey | 13. Frugal | 21. Flotilla |
| 6. Funicular | 14. Felicitous | 22. Frivolous |
| 7. Fatuous | 15. Foreboding | 23. Fortitude |
| 8. Formidable | 16. Fraternize | 24. Flexible |

### Rare Words • 1 (page 46)

1. becoming fatty
2. hooked, curved inward
3. growing or passing into white
4. sand-loving
5. public disgrace
6. given to drinking

7. pertaining to a trumpeter or trumpeting
8. shaped like a spur
9. the hypnotic state in animals when they "sham dead"
10. growing in tufts or clumps, turfy
11. the disposition of light and shade in a painting
12. the art of gesticulation in oratory
13. the scar of a healed wound
14. an ancient type of water-clock
15. wasting away, atrophied
16. pertaining to twilight, dim, indistinct
17. melting away, becoming liquid
18. the action of stretching apart, spreading out, divergence
19. an egg-hatching apparatus
20. without front teeth
21. relating to or supported by alms or alms-giving
22. having no eyebrows
23. bleeding from the nose
24. flowing with gall
25. having a border or fringe
26. reproducing by fission
27. having the form of a rope or cord
28. a person who eats earth
29. one who defines terms, one versed in the science of language
30. of the nature of gum, gum-like
31. the worship of saints
32. a great public sacrifice
33. having teeth all of the same kind
34. violet-colored
35. a person's private mark or signature
36. incapable of mixture e.g. water and oil

**Congratulations! You've finished the first seven days!**

# DAY EIGHT

## PHOBIAS

A *phobia* is a fear or dread of some particular thing. To what do these phobias apply?

1. Agoraphobia
2. Bathophobia
3. Claustrophobia
4. Cynophobia
5. Ergophobia
6. Gynophobia
7. Nyctophobia
8. Phobophobia
9. Phonophobia
10. Scopophobia
11. Xenophobia
12. Zoophobia

## MANIAS

A *mania* is a compulisve desire or craze for something. can you say what things are desired by people with these manias?

1. Agromania
2. Bibliomania
3. Chirablutomania
4. Chronomania
5. Dipsomania
6. Dromomania
7. Kleptomania
8. Megalomania
9. Metromania
10. Nostomania
11. Pyromania
12. Sophomania

## ILLNESSES

The following are all diseases or ailments of the body. Do you know which part of the body they each affect?

1. Arthritis
2. Bronchitis
3. Colitis
4. Conjunctivitis
5. Dermatitis
6. Gastritis
7. Hepatitis
8. Meningitis
9. Neuritis
10. Phlebitis
11. Poliomyelitis
12. Stomatitis

## ADJECTIVES • 1

Adjectives are useful words for describing things and people. Define the following adjectives.

1. Anomalous

2. Bicameral

3. Captious

4. Crass

5. Dubious

6. Exotic

7. Fulsome

8. Grandiose

9. Halcyon

10. Humorous

11. Impassive

12. Leprous

13. Macabre

14. Magniloquent

15. Narcotic

16. Obese

17. Prevalent

18. Puerile

19. Repugnant

20. Spurious

21. Sagacious

22. Tawny

23. Vibrant

24. Wary

25. Abysmal

26. Bilingual

27. Bloated

28. Congenial

29. Dispassionate

30. Exorbitant

31. Fallacious

32. Gaunt

33. Hypercritical

34. Hackneyed

35. Impious

36 Lukewarm

## COMPLETE THE WORD CHALLENGE • G

Complete the following words from the given meanings.

1. Gn _ _ s _  a type of rock
2. G _ _ _ t _ n _ _ s  jelly-like
3. G _ as _ l _  horrible, frightful
4. G _ _ m _ _ _ t _  to sprout or bud
5. G _ _ d _ _ _ t  degree of slope
6. G _ _ f _ _  coarse laughter
7. G _ _ n _ s _  to decorate, embellish
8. G _ r _ _ n _ _ _ n  enormous, gigantic
9. G _ _ b _ _ _  convex, hump-shaped
10. G _ _ _ l _ n  imaginary mischievous sprite or elf
11. G _ _ _ o _ a  type of boat
12. G _ l _ _ n _ t _  type of explosive
13. Gn _ _ l _ _  twisted, rugged, knobbly
14. G _ _ b _ _ _  a small round drop (of liquid)
15. G _ w _ _  awkward, ungainly
16. G _ _ _ r _ _ _ _ y  the art of good eating
17. G _ _ _ _ a _ _  one who has a degree
18. G _ _ f _ _ t _  writing scratched on walls
19. Go _ _ _ m _ _  a filmy substance made of spiders' webs
20. G _ _ e _ te _ _  a geographical dictionary
21. G _ r _ a _ _  relevant or pertinent
22. G _ s _ _ c _ l _ _ _  to motion or gesture with the limbs
23. Gl _ _ _ _ _ y  a list of words or dictionary
24. G _ u _ o _ _  a type of sugar

# DAY NINE

## COMPLETE THE WORD CHALLENGE • H

Complete the following words from the given meanings.

1. H _ _ _ _ d _ _ s  risky, perilous
2. H _ _ e _ _ s  repulsive, revolting
3. H _ _ t _ l _ _ _  antagonism, opposition
4. H _ l _ _ _ l  spiral
5. H _ r _ _ r  place of shelter
6. Ha _ _ n _ _ e  to address or speak loudly and vehemently
7. H _ l _ _ _ d  a combined spear and battle-axe
8. H _ _ i _ o _ _ e _  a kind of aircraft
9. H _ e _ o _ _ _ p _ _ c  an ancient form of writing
10. H _ _ s _ _ _ d  old liquid measure
11. H _ p _ a _ _ r _  chance, random
12. H _ _ _ c _ _ s _  pretence, simulation of virtue
13. H _ _ i _ _ t _ _ _  indecision, reluctance
14. H _ _ i _ _ d _  the killing of a human being
15. H _ _ ch _ _ _ t  escutcheon, armorial shield
16. H _ l _ c _ _ _ t  wholesale destruction or slaughter
17. H _ _ _ r _ ou _  mirthful, joyous
18. H _ _ _ _ n _ _ e  to sleep through the winter
19. H _ _ m _ _ i _ _ s  agreeable, concordant
20. H _ _ d _ _ _ g  precipitate, impetuous
21. H _ _ _ o _ _  type of hanging bed
22. H _ n _ _ _ n _ _  obstruction, obstacle
23. H _ b _ _ d  offspring of two different species
24. H _ _ e _ s _ _ _  type of canvas carrying-bag

# TEST YOUR VOCABULARY • H-I
### Define the following words:

37. Hirsute

38. Homily

39. Homogeneous

40. Hone

41. Honorarium

42. Horripilation

43. Howitzer

44. Humid

45. Hydropathy

46. Hyphen

47. Hypochondriac

48. Hypotenuse

49. Iconoclast

50. Idiosyncrasy

51. Ignominy

52. Ignoramus

53. Illimitable

54. Imbroglio

55. Immanent

56. Immure

57. Impale

58. Impasse

59. Impecunious

60. Imperturbable

61. Incarcerated

62. Inchoate

63. Indigenous

64. Ineluctable

65. Infringe

66. Inimical

67. Integument

68. Interpolate

69. Inveterate

70. Inviolate

71. Irascible

72. Irrevocable

## A LANGUAGE OF THEIR OWN

Most fields of human activity have a peculiar terminology, not always understood by the layman.

Can you say in which sports, hobbies, professions or
interests these groups of terms are used? (You're not asked
to provide their definitions.)

1. gules, argent, akimbo, rampant
2. option, placing, yield , bull
3. chinaman, gully, cover, yorker
4. foxing, impression, calf, marbled
5. spandrel, tympanum, clerestory, metope
6. occlusion, adiabatic, supercooled, isohyet
7. rallentando, sostenuto, diapason, breve
8. chert, Jurassic, porphyry, hornblende
9. catalyst, litmus, colloidal, precipitate
10. mashie, eagle, spoon, dormy
11. stadia, offset, resection, triangulation
12. perforated, mint, overprint, watermark
13. mulching, cloche, dibber, rust
14. reprise, flèche, coquille, tierce
15. focal length, rangefinder, cassette, condenser
16. binomial, quadratic, secant, mantissa
17. gouache, tempera, filbert, mahlstick
18. lynchet, fogou, cursus, megalith
19. face off, puck, penalty bench, alley
20. subliminal, schizoid, Rorschach, ambiversion
21. spinnaker, luff up, shrouds, pushpit
22. soubresaut, hortensia, épaulement, entrechat
23. macramé, picots, tatting, one passing
24. quatrain, hexameter, distich, anapaest

# DAY TEN

## "-OLOGIES"

Zoology is the science of the study of animals. To which branches of science or knowledge do these apply?

1. Algology
2. Barology
3. Carpology
4. Cardiology
5. Dendrology
6. Entomology
7. Ethnology
8. Etymology
9. Gerontology
10. Graphology
11. Herpetology
12. Hypnology
13. Ichthyology
14. Metrology
15. Odontology
16. Oology
17. Ornithology
18. Otology
19. Philology
20. Paleontology
21. Rhinology
22. Speleology
23. Toxicology
24. Vulcanology

## "-METERS"

The suffix *-meter* is derived from the Latin *-metrum-* measure. What do these instruments measure?

1. Altimeter
2. Ammeter
3. Anemometer
4. Bathometer
5. Calorimeter
6. Chronometer
7. Clinometer
8. Dasymeter
9. Echometer
10. Galvanometer
11. Goniometer
12. Hyetometer
13. Hygrometer
14. Lactometer
15. Macrometer
16. Micrometer
17. Manometer
18. Optometer
19. Opisometer
20. Pedometer
21. Photometer
22. Pyrometer
23. Seismometer
24. Tachometer

## COMPLETE THE WORD CHALLENGE • I

Complete the following words from the given meanings.

1. I _ m _ _ _ l _ t _  pure, spotless, faultless
2. I _ c _ _ s _ _ t  unceasing, continual
3. I _ _ r _ d _ c _ _ _ _  that which cannot be got rid of
4. I _ _ n _ _ _ r _  a route or guide-book
5. I _ _ _ st _ _ _ us  distinguished, famous
6. In _ _ _ s _ _ _ r _ _ _  thoughtless, regardless of others
7. In _ _ _ n _ _ g _ _ t  uncompromising, unmoved
8. I _ m _ _ ab _ _  unalterable, unchangeable
9. I _ _ _ n _ r _ _ _  to burn, reduce to ashes
10. I _ l _ s _ _ e  deceptive
11. I _ s _ _ s _ _ _  unfeeling, without sensation
12. I _ _ or _ _ _ _ te  persistent, pressing
13. I _ _ _ b _ _ _  motionless
14. I _ h _ b _ _ _ n _  one living in a place, resident
15. I _ _ r _ _ c _ l _ _ _  not jointed, unable to speak clearly
16. I _ m _ n _ _ _  impending, soon to occur
17. In _ _ d _ _ i _ _ _  unwise, ill-judged
18. I _ g _ _ t _ _ _ _  to get oneself into favor with
19. I _ p _ _ c _ _ l _  faultless
20. I _ s _ _ _ d  tasteless, lifeless
21. I _ _ u _ _ _ d _ n _ _ _  disobedient, rebellious
22. I _ _ _ m _ t _ _ l _  unyielding, stubborn
23. I _ v _ _ _ l _  to entice or seduce
24. I _ _ er _ ec _ _ _ _  a fault or blemish

## VERBS • 2

The precise use of verbs is essential to good English. Define this second group of verbs.

| | |
|---|---|
| 37. Malign | 55. Frustrate |
| 38. Masquerade | 56. Grangerize |
| 39. Nominate | 57. Glimmer |
| 40. Occlude | 58. Incriminate |
| 41. Perpetrate | 59. Instigate |
| 42. Pertain | 60. Loiter |
| 43. Rifle | 61. Meditate |
| 44. Scurry | 62. Molest |
| 45. Simulate | 63. Nurture |
| 46. Terminate | 64. Palliate |
| 47. Vilify | 65. Placate |
| 48. Vitiate | 66. Propitiate |
| 49. Advocate | 67. Recoup |
| 50. Berate | 68. Supplicate |
| 51. Converge | 69. Subjugate |
| 52. Castigate | 70. Transmogrify |
| 53. Delegate | 71. Underrate |
| 54. Evince | 72. Verify |

# DAY ELEVEN

## STRANGE WORDS • 1

There are some very strange words in the English language. Here are a few of them, some familiar and some not so familiar. How many do you know the meaning of?

1. Abracadabra
2. Alalia
3. Apoplexy
4. Balderdash
5. Bigwig
6. Blunderbuss
7. Blurb
8. Breastsummer
9. Calliope
10. Cantankerous
11. Circumbendibus
12. Collywobbles
13. Congeries
14. Coxcomb
15. Dumdum
16. Factotum
17. Feoffee
18. Fidibus
19. Fizgig
20. Flapdoodle
21. Flibbertigibbet
22. Flim-flam
23. Galactagogue
24. Gazebo
25. Gewgaw
26. Ginkgo
27. Goatling
28. Grog-blossom
29. Hippophagy
30. Hobbledehoy
31. Hullabaloo
32. Ignicolist
33. Jackanapes
34. Jocoserious
35. Knicker-bockers
36. Lapis-lazuli

## ODD WORD OUT • 2

In each of the following groups all the words except one have approximately the same meaning. Which is the odd word out in each group and what is its meaning?

1. Genuine, inimitable, authentic, true
2. Impromptu, ready, prepared, available
3. Appoint, ordain, direct, proscribe
4. Crowd, multitude, conclave, throng
5. Urge, advocate, augment, stimulate
6. Clever, austere, skilful, talented
7. Hallucination, apparition, delusion, allusion
8. Onus, ownership, possession, control
9. Intrepid, dangerous, risky, hazardous
10. Intelligence, lucidity, celerity, logic
11. Culpable, feckless, blameworthy, guilty
12. Extravagance, wastefulness, prodigality, largesse
13. Thought, idea, reflection, penchant
14. Amusing, comical, adroit, wry
15. Argument, tenet, discussion, debate
16. Temporal, limited, transient, ephemeral
17. Container, vase, shard, urn
18. Careless, negligent, thoughtless, prolix
19. Conceited, protuberant, vain, opinionated
20. Incline, proclivity, gradient, slope
21. Quixotic, comical, laughable, humorous
22. Quiet, peace, solace, calm
23. Secret, concealed, hidden, insidious
24. Humility, demeanor. meekness, unpretentiousness

## COMPLETE THE WORD CHALLENGE • L

Complete the following words from the given meanings.

1. Li _ _ id _ _ _ to wipe out, get rid of
2. L _ n _ _ v _ _ _ long life
3. L _ d _ _ r _ _ _ absurd, ridiculous
4. Le _ _ e _ _ tolerant, gentle
5. Lo _ t _ _ _ m _ sickening, repulsive
6. L _ _ e _ _ c _ ability to read and write
7. Le _ _ t _ t _ to make something rise in the air
8. L _ _ _ l _ u _ a type of floor-covering
9. L _ s _ _ _ u _ e weariness
10. L _ _ c _ _ _ s excessively sweet, cloying
11. Li _ _ i _ _ a type of brown coal
12. L _ _ _ n _ _ s shining, bright, giving light
13. L _ c _ _ t _ _ n _ growing in or relating to lakes
14. Lu _ _ a _ _ v _ gainful, profitable
15. L _ t _ _ r _ _ on or by the shore
16. L _ _ r _ c _ _ e to make smooth, apply oil or grease
17. L _ _ h _ supple, flexible
18. L _ _ _ r _ _ e to set free or release
19. L _ u _ _ b _ _ commendable, praiseworthy
20. L _ _ e _ _ c _ a nonsense verse of five lines
21. Lu _ u _ r _ t _ _ _ nocturnal study or meditation
22. L _ p _ d _ _ _ a cutter or polisher of gems
23. L _ _ _ nt _ _ _ _ deplorable, regrettable
24. L _ c _ _ _ c brief, concise

# DAY TWELVE

## GEOGRAPHY AND GEOLOGY

Define the following words, all of which you may come across in the course of normal reading.

1. Anticyclone
2. Archipelago
3. Basalt
4. Col
5. Delta
6. Drumlin
7. Equinox
8. Fiord
9. Glacier
10. Isobar
11. Isthmus
12. Lava
13. Meridian
14. Monsoon
15. Moraine
16. Orthomorphic
17. Rhumb-line
18. Scarp
19. Scree
20. Solstice
21. Stalactite
22. Theodolite
23. Tundra
24. Watershed

## BIOLOGY, BOTANY AND ZOOLOGY

1. Aorta
2. Carnivore
3. Cartilage
4. Chlorophyll
5. Chromosomes
6. Clavicle
7. Coniferous
8. Deciduous
9. Epidermis
10. Gene
11. Haemoglobin
12. Hormone
13. Latex
14. Metabolism
15. Mollusc
16. Penicillin
17. Plankton
18. Plasma
19. Pollen
20. Protoplasm
21. Stamen
22. Tendril
23. Tuber
24. Vitamin

## COMPLETE THE WORD CHALLENGE • M

Complete the following words from the given meanings.

1. M _ d _ _ c _ _  middling, indifferent
2. M _ _ d _ m _ _ n _ _  an offence or misdeed
3. Mo _ o _ o _ _ _  a speech by, or scene for, one person
4. M _ _ _ m _ _ p _ _ s _  to change the nature or form of
5. Mo _ o _ _  sullen, gloomy
6. M _ _ _ _ p  an unlucky accident
7. M _ l _ _ _ c _ _ _ n  a curse
8. M _ ll _ _ _  to appease or soften
9. M _ _ l _ _ _ _ m  a large whirlpool
10. M _ _ i _ _ p _ l  of local government
11. M _ l _ _ _ h _ l _  sadness, depression
12. M _ r _ _ _ t _ _  type of inlaid work
13. M _ _ t _ t _ _ e  a large gathering or crowd
14. M _ _ r _ c _ _ _  representation in miniature, epitome
15. M _ n _ _ _ l _ _ _  to handle, manage with skill
16. Me _ _ t _ r _ _ _ s  deserving of reward or praise
17. M _ _ st _ _  a large church or cathedral
18. M _ n _ _ c _ l _  very small (especially script)
19. M _ n _ _ _ n _ _ s  lacking variety
20. M _ s _ _ c _ _  slaughter, carnage
21. Ma _ e _ _ a _ i _ e  to cause to appear, to make a fact
22. M _ _ z _ _ _ n _  a low story between two high ones
23. M _ _ d _ _ _ n _  a beggar
24. M _ u _ o _ e _ _  a magnificent tomb

## TEST YOUR VOCABULARY • L-M

Define the following words:

1. Lackadaisical
2. Lampoon
3. Languid
4. Lectern
5. Leeward
6. Legerdemain
7. Lentitude
8. Lethargy
9. Lexicography
10. Ligneous
11. Limbo
12. Limpid
13. Lineage
14. Lissom
15. Lithium
16. Litigate
17. Loggia
18. Loquacious
19. Loxodrome
20 Lucid
21. Lugubrious
22. Lunate
23. Lusty
24. Luxuriate
25. Machinate
26. Magnanimous
27. Maladroit
28. Maleficent
29. Marquee
30. Masticate
31. Mellifluous
32. Mendacious
33. Mercurial
34. Meretricious
35. Meticulous
36. Minatory

# DAY THIRTEEN

## THE PRECISE WORD

Knowing the one and only word which exactly fits a given definition is a valuable asset. Can you name the words which fit these definitions?

1. The class of mammals which carry their young in a pouch.
2. Wreckage found floating on the surface of the sea.
3. The art of paper-folding.
4. A word or sentence that reads the same backwards and forwards.
5. Goods thrown overboard to lighten a ship.
6. A legendary animal with the head and wings of an eagle and the body of a lion.
7. An exaggerated statement not meant to be taken literally.
8. The rearing of silkworms for producing raw silk.
9. Fortune-telling by means of playing-cards.
10. Talking in one's sleep.
11. Living both on land and in water.
12. A two-hundredth anniversary
13. The collecting of postage-stamps
14. The study of coins.
15. A small lizard which can change its color.
16. A case for holding arrows.
17. A pair of eyeglasses with a spring which clips the nose.
18. A rain-water spout in the form of a grotesque human or animal head.
19. The killing of one's own brother.
20. The smallest pig of a litter.
21. An English word for a device intended to aid the memory.
22. The nesting-lace of a swarm of bees.
23. A group of six persons or things.
24. The science of projectiles.

## ADJECTIVES • 2

Adjectives are useful words for describing things and people. Define the following adjectives.

37. Minute

38. Malleable

39. Nomadic

40. Olfactory

41. Phlegmatic

42. Querulous

43. Restive

44. Susceptible

45. Sombre

46. Tangible

47. Vicarious

48. Veracious

49. Arduous

50. Benign

51. Cogent

52. Cursory

53. Deferential

54. Euphonious

55. Flaccid

56. Glutinous

57. Histrionic

58. Impetuous

59. Jocose

60. Listless

61. Mawkish

62. Militant

63. Noxious

64. Omniscient

65. Pedantic

66. Prodigious

67. Queasy

68. Sentient

69. Stentorian

70. Tactile

71. Verbose

72. Worldly

## COMPLETE THE WORD CHALLENGE • N

Complete the following words from the given meanings.

1. N _ g _ l _ _ g  trifling, petty
2. No _ o _ _ o _ _  well-known, talked of
3. No _ _ _ m _  harmful, objectionable
4. N _ n _ _ s _ _ _ p _  not easily described or classified
5. N _ t _ t _  to droop
6. N _ t _ _ r _ _ _ k  a species of toad
7. N _ _ r _ g _ _  a common gas
8. N _ g _ _ c _  to omit to do, pay no attention to
9. N _ _ t _ _ _ _ l  of or by night
10. N _ u _ e _ u _  offensive, nasty, disgusting
11. N _ c _ _  a recess in a wall
12. N _ o _ i _ _ _ c  relating to the late Stone Age
13. N _ c _ _ r _ _ e  a kind of peach
14. N _ d _ _ _  a small rounded lump
15. Na _ _ _ a _ e  to sail, direct the course of
16. N _ tr _ _ _ n _  nourishing food
17. N _ n _ n _ _ _ y  a non-existent thing, figment
18. N _ _ _ l _ _ m  negative doctrines in religion
19. N _ t _ _ k _  Japanese carved ornament
20. N _ _ o _ _ n _  a constituent of tobacco
21. N _ _ g _ b _ rh _ _ _  nearness, vicinity of
22. N _ _ e _ s _ _ _  indispensable, needful
23. N _ r _ _ l _ _ _ y  inclination to fall asleep
24. N _ _ _ r  the lowest point of anything

# TEST YOUR VOCABULARY • M-N

Define the following words:

37. Mischance

38. Misogynist

39. Mitigate

40. Modulate

41. Monitory

42. Mordant

43. Moribund

44. Multifarious

45. Munificent

46. Muslin

47. Mutilate

48. Myriad

49. Naïve

50. Narcissism

51. Natation

52. Nebulous

53. Necromancy

54. Nefarious

55. Negate

56. Negligible

57. Neophyte

58. Nephology

59. Nescient

60. Nexus

61. Nidificate

62. Niggardly

63. Nomenclature

64. Nonchalant

65. Nonpareil

66. Nostalgia

67. Nostrum

68. Notional

69. Novercal

70. Nuance

71. Nugatory

72. Nullify

# DAY FOURTEEN

## SOMETHING IN COMMON

The words in each of the following groups are closely related or have something in common. Can you say what it is?

1. palladium, ytterbium, dysprosium, arsenic
2. bilharzia, beriberi, thrush, shingles
3. sackbut, serpent, ophicleide, rebec
4. saltarello, tarantella, seguidilla, schottische
5. cirrus, cumulus, stratus, nimbus
6. prolepsis, anacoluthon, zeugma, diaeresis
7. sombrero, fedora, kepi, fez
8. felucca, sampan, ketch, dhow
9. chinook, mistral, sirocco, khamsin
10. brougham, phaeton, landau, cabriolet
11. savannah, steppe, pampas, prairie
12. barbican, postern, bailey, portcullis
13. kale, kohlrabi, broccoli, artichoke
14. adze, awl, gimlet, plane
15. riesling, hock, sauternes, tokay
16. escritoire, davenport, whatnot, commode
17. vermouth, benedictine, chartreuse, absinth
18. melinite, lyddite, cordite, guncotton
19. coulomb, joule, henry, farad
20. gamboge, sienna, vermilion, indigo
21. lacrosse, fives, shinty, hurling
22. samoyed, borzoi, saluki, chihuahua
23. cuirass, pauldron, greave, gorget
24. cantilever, swing, bascule, transporter

## RARE WORDS • 2

Many words are seldom used in everyday language. Here are some of these uncommon words; most of them however have simpler and more straightforward meanings than many common words. If you get three or more definitions correct, give yourself a pat on the back!

37. Impudicity
38. Incalescent
39. Incondite
40. Lactifluous
41. Latifoliate
42. Lucifugous
43. Monoculous
44. Multiloquence
45. Nephrotomy
46. Nuncupate
47. Obfuscate
48. Obliviscence
49. Pentadactyl
50. Peristeronic
51. Plumiform
52. Polyonymous
53. Revirescence
54. Rhyparographer

55. Sciopticon
56. Securiform
57. Senocular
58. Sternutation
59. Strabismus
60. Strigose
61. Supellectile
62. Tabescent
63. Tephromancy
64. Tenebrosity
65. Tralatitious
66. Triphthong
67. Urticate
68. Uxoricide
69. Vespertine
70. Vicegerent
71. Volitate
72. Zymurgy

# WEEK TWO ANSWERS

## - DAY EIGHT ANSWERS -

### Phobias (page 66)

1. open or public places
2. falling from a height
3. enclosed spaces
4. dogs
5. being active
6. women
7. darkness or night
8. being afraid
9. certain sounds
10. being stared at
11. strangers
12. animals

### Manias (page 66)

1. to be alone
2. to collect books
3. excessive handwashing
4. perfectionism in timekeeping
5. alcohol
6. to wander
7. to steal
8. to have great power
9. to compose verse
10. longing for home
11. to start fires
12. belief in one's own wisdom

### Illnesses (page 66)

1. joints
2. lungs
3. colon or intestines
4. eye
5. skin
6. stomach
7. liver
8. brain and spinal cord
9. nerves
10. veins
11. spinal cord
12. mouth

### Adjectives • 1 (page 67)

1. abnormal, unconformable, irregular
2. having two chambers
3. fond of fault-finding or raising objections
4. grossly stupid, insensitive, dense
5. doubting, hesitating, uncertain
6. strange, unusual, foreign
7. over-demonstrative, offensively excessive
8. impressive, imposing, pompous
9. calm, peaceful, happy
10. full of humor, comical, facetious
11. devoid of feeling or emotion, imperturbable
12. afflicted with leprosy
13. grim, gruesome
14. lofty or ambitious in expression, boastful
15. inducing sleep or drowsiness
16. fat, fleshy, corpulent
17. frequently occurring, in general use, predominant
18. childish, immature, trivial
19. distasteful, objectionable, contradictory
20. not genuine, false, sham, counterfeit
21. discerning, shrewd, having good judgement
22. of orange-brown color
23. vibrating, quivering rapidly, resonant
24. cautious, careful, circumspect
25. bottomless, extremely bad
26. having or speaking two languages
27. swollen, of excessive size, pampered
28. suited or agreeable to, of the same temperament
29. free from emotion, calm, composed, impartial
30. excessive, outrageously large
31. deceptive, misleading, delusive

32. lean, haggard, grim, desolate
33. over-critical, excessively fault-finding
34. trite, stale, commonplace
35. irreverent, irreligious, wicked
36. moderately warm, tepid

### Cmplete the Word Challenge • G (page 68)

| | | |
|---|---|---|
| 1. Gneiss | 9. Gibbous | 17. Graduate |
| 2. Gelatinous | 10. Gremlin | 18. Graffiti |
| 3. Ghastly | 11. Gondola | 19. Gossamer |
| 4. Germinate | 12. Gelignite | 20. Gazetteer |
| 5. Gradient | 13. Gnarled | 21. Germane |
| 6. Guffaw | 14. Globule | 22. Gesticulate |
| 7. Garnish | 15. Gawky | 23. Glossary |
| 8. Gargantuan | 16. Gastronomy | 24. Glucose |

## - DAY NINE -

### Complete the Word Challenge • H (page 70)

| | | |
|---|---|---|
| 1. Hazardous | 9. Hieroglyphic | 17. Hilarious |
| 2. Hideous | 10. Hogshead | 18. Hibernate |
| 3. Hostility | 11. Haphazard | 19. Harmonious |
| 4. Helical | 12. Hypocrisy | 20. Headlong |
| 5. Harbor | 13. Hesitation | 21. Hammock |
| 6. Harangue | 14. Homicide | 22. Hindrance |
| 7. Halberd | 15. Hatchment | 23. Hybrid |
| 8. Helicopter | 16. Holocaust | 24. Haversack |

### Test Your Vocabulary • H-I (page 71)

37. relating to hair, hairy, shaggy
38. a sermon, lecture, tedious moralizing discourse
39. of the same kind, alike, similar, uniform
40. a stone for sharpening tools
41. an honorary reward, fee for services rendered
42. creeping of the flesh, "goose-flesh"

43. a gun which fires heavy shells
44. moist, damp
45. medical treatment by application of water
46. a dash used to connect two words
47. depression without cause, or by unfounded belief of bodily disease
48. the side opposite the right angle of a triangle
49. a breaker of images, one who attacks cherished beliefs
50. mental constitution peculiar to a person, individual bent
51. dishonor, disgrace, infamy
52. an ignorant person
53. that which has no limits, boundless
54. confused heap, complicated situation, misunderstanding
55. indwelling, inherent
56. to imprison, confine within walls, shut oneself up
57. to thrust a stake through
58. a blind alley, a way with no outlet
59. penniless, in need of money
60. not excitable, serene, calm
61. imprisoned, confined
62. undeveloped, immature, just begun; (verb) to begin
63. native, belonging naturally, innate
64. inescapable
65. to break or violate, to contravene
66. unfriendly or hostile to, harmful
67. a skin, husk, shell, natural covering of animal or plant
68. to make insertions (in books, etc.), introduce or insert terms
69. long-established, deep-rooted, hardened, settled, obstinate
70. unhurt, unbroken, unprofaned, not violated
71. prone to anger, irritable, choleric
72. unalterable, irreversible, beyond recall

## A Language of Their Own (page 72)

1. Heraldry
2. Stockbroking
3. Cricket
4. Book collecting
5. Architecture
6. Meteorology
7. Music
8. Geology
9. Chemistry
10. Golf
11. Land surveying
12. Philately
13. Gardening
14. Fencing
15. Photography
16. Mathematics
17. Art
18. Archaeology
19. Ice Hockey
20. Psychology
21. Sailing
22. Ballet
23. Needlework
24. Poetry

## - DAY TEN -

### "-Ologies" (page 74)

1. Algae or seaweeds
2. Weight
3. Fruits
4. The heart
5. Trees
6. Insects
7. Races of mankind
8. Origin of words
9. Old age
10. Character from handwriting
11. Reptiles
12. Sleep
13. Fishes
14. Weights and measures
15. Teeth
16. Birds' eggs
17. Birds
18. Ears and diseases of the ear
19. Language
20. Fossils
21 The nose
22. Caves
23. Poisons
24. Volcanoes

### "-Meters" (page 74)

1. Altitude
2. Electric currents
3. Wind speed
4. Depth of water
5. Amount of heat or specific heat
6. Time
7. Slopes and altitudes
8. Density of gases
9. Duration of sounds
10. Electric (galvanic) currents
11. Angles
12. Rainfall
13. Humidity of air of gas
14. Specific gravity or purity of milk
15. Distant objects
16. Small objects, small distances
17. Elastic force of gases
18. Eyesight
19. Lines and distances on a map
20. Distance travelled on foot
21. Intensity of light
22. High temperatures
23. Earthquakes
24. Velocity of machines or of water

## Complete the Word Challenge • I (page 75)

1. Immaculate
2. Incessant
3. Ineradicable
4. Itinerary
5. Illustrious
6. Inconsiderate
7. Intransigent
8. Immutable
9. Incinerate
10. Illusive
11. Insensate
12. Importunate
13. Immobile
14. Inhabitant
15. Inarticulate
16. Imminent
17. Injudicious
18. Ingratiate
19. Impeccable
20. Insipid
21. Insubordinate
22. Indomitable
23. Inveigle
24. Imperfection

## Verbs • 2 (page 76)

37. speak ill of, slander
38. appear in disguise or as false character
39. name, fix, specify, appoint, designate
40. obstruct, stop up, shut in
41. perform, execute, commit
42. belong, relate to, be appropriate to
43. plunder, ransack, pillage, despoil
44. move rapidly or hastily
45. feign, pretend, imitate
46. bring or come to an end, bound or limit
47. defame, speak evil of
48. impair, spoil, invalidate
49. recommend, argue in favour of
50. scold
51. come together, approach, tend to meet in a point
52. punish or rebuke severely
53. depute, entrust, commission as deputy
54. indicate, make evident or manifest
55. baffle, defeat, foil
56. illustrate book with extra prints or engravings
57. shine faintly, give a faint light

58. charge with a crime, involve in accusation
59. urge on, stir up, provoke
60. linger, hang about, travel indolently
61. contemplate, exercise the mind in thought
62. meddle with a person with hostile intent
63. nourish, rear, bring up, foster
64. alleviate, mitigate, ease
65. pacify, conciliate, make friendly
66. appease, conciliate
67. make up for, make good, recover
68. beg, entreat humbly
69. subdue, bring under control or bondage
70. alter form or appearance, transform
71. underestimate, assess too low
72. confirm, demonstrate or check truth of

## - DAY ELEVEN -

### Strange Words • 1 (page 78)

1. a spell, magic word or formula, gibberish
2. loss of speech
3. a malady which arrests the powers of sense and motion
4. a meaningless jumble of words
5. a man of high office or importance
6. a short gun with a large bore which fires many slugs
7. a publisher's advertisement for a book
8. a beam over a large opening which holds up the super structure
9. a musical instrument with steam-whistles and a keyboard
10. quarrelsome, cross-grained
11. a roundabout method, circumlocution
12. pain or rumbling in the intestines
13. a collection or mass of things heaped together

14. a foolish, conceited person
15. a type of bullet
16. a man of all-work, a servant who manages his master's affairs
17. a person to whom freehold estate is conveyed by feoffment
18. a paper spill for lighting a candle or pipe
19. a flighty woman, a kind of firework
20. nonsense talk
21. a gossip or flighty woman
22. nonsense, humbug, deception
23. anything which induces a flow of milk
24. a small building or room, usually in a garden, erected to obtain a view
25. a gaudy toy or bauble, a showy trifle
26. a Japanese tree, also known as the maidenhair-tree
27. a goat over one year and under two years old
28. a redness of the nose caused by excessive drinking
29. the practice of eating horse-flesh
30. a clumsy or awkward youth between boyhood and manhood
31. a tumultuous noise, uproar
32. a fire-worshipper
33. an upstart or impertinent fellow
34. half jocular, half serious
35. type of loose-fitting breeches
36. a bright blue silicate and pigment

### Odd Word Out • 2 (page 79)

1. Inimitable - defying imitation, peerless
2. Impromptu - without preparation, improvised
3. Proscribe - denounce, banish, condemn, prohibit
4. Conclave - secret council, close assembly
5. Augment - increase, add to
6. Austere - severely simple, strict, grave

7. Allusion - indirect or implied reference
8. Onus - burden, charge, responsibility
9. Intrepid - fearless, daring, brave
10. Celerity - swiftness, speed
11. Feckless - ineffective, futile, weak
12. Largesse - generous or liberal gift
13. Penchant - inclination, bias, bent
14. Adroit - dexterous, clever, skilful
15. Tenet - opinion, dogma, doctrine
16. Temporal - worldly, earthly
17. Shard - fragment, broken piece of earthenware
18. Prolix - long-winded, tedious, wordy
19. Protuberant - bulging, sticking out, prominent
20. Proclivity - tendency, inclination, leaning
21. Quixotic - visionary, idealistic
22. Solace - comfort, consolation
23. Insidious - sly, deceitful, artful, cunning
24. Demeanor - behavior, bearing, conduct

### Complete the Word Challenge • L (page 80)

1. Liquidate
2. Longevity
3. Ludicrous
4. Lenient
5. Loathsome
6. Literacy
7. Levitate
8. Linoleum
9. Lassitude
10. Luscious
11. Lignite
12. Luminous
13. Lacustrine
14. Lucrative
15. Littoral
16. Lubricate
17. Lithe
18. Liberate
19. Laudable
20. Limerick
21. Lucubration
22. Lapidary
23. Lamentable
24. Laconic

## - DAY TWELVE -

### Geography and Geology (page 82)

1. an area of relatively high pressure, with settled weather
2. a scattered group of islands
3. a type of volcanic rock (the Giant's Causeway is basalt)
4. a depression or low point in a mountain range, providing a pass across
5. an alluvial area at the mouth of a river
6. a low, elongated hill formed of material deposited by a glacier
7. the time of the year when the sun is directly overhead at noon at the Equator
8. a long, deep, narrow inlet of the sea (as in Norway)
9. a large mass of ice moving slowly down a valley
10. a line on a map joining places with equal barometric pressure
11. a neck of land connecting two land areas, with water either side
12. molten rock which has solidified on the earth's surface
13. a line of Longitude
14. the seasonal winds in south-east Asia, also the rains which accompany these winds
15. the material deposited by a glacier
16. a type of map projection which preserves the shape of small areas
17. a line of constant bearing, cutting meridians at the same angle
18. the steep slope of a line of hills or ridge
19. a mass of boulders and stones which lies at the foot of a hill
20. the time of the year when the sun is directly overhead at the Tropics
21. a column of calcium carbonate hanging from the roof of a limestone cave
22. a surveying instrument used for measuring angles
23. the treeless plains of the subarctic regions
24. the line which separates streams flowing into different river basins

## Biology, Botany and Zoology (page 82)

1. the large artery leading from the left ventricle of the heart
2. a flesh-eating mammal
3. the skeletal tissue in vertebrate animals
4. the green coloring matter in the cells of plants
5. small bodies in the nuclei of living cells
6. the collar-bone of a human
7. the type of trees which produce cones
8. the trees which shed their leaves every year
9. the outer layer of the skin of animals
10. a unit of inherited material or a hereditary factor
11. the pigment in the blood of vertebrates and a few other animals
12. a chemical substance produced by certain glands
13. a milky fluid produced by some plants and trees e.g. rubber
14. the chemical processes or changes occurring within an organism
15. an animal with a hard shell e.g. oyster, snail
16. an antibiotic obtained from a vegetable mold
17. microscopic animal and plant life near the surface of lake or sea
18. the liquid in which blood corpuscles float
19. the spores of plants
20. the living material of the cells of all organisms
21. the stalk-shaped organ of a flower which produces pollen
22. a modified stem or leaf which a plant uses for support
23. an underground root or stem, swollen with stored food
24. an organic substance found in many foods and necessary for life

## Complete the Word Challenge • M (page 83)

| | | |
|---|---|---|
| 1. Mediocre | 9. Maelstrom | 17. Minster |
| 2. Misdemeanor | 10. Municipal | 18. Minuscule |
| 3. Monologue | 11. Melancholy | 19. Monotonous |
| 4. Metamorphose | 12. Marquetry | 20. Massacre |
| 5. Morose | 13. Multitude | 21. Materialize |
| 6. Mishap | 14. Microcosm | 22. Mezzanine |
| 7. Malediction | 15. Manipulate | 23. Mendicant |
| 8. Mollify | 16. Meritorious | 24. Mausoleum |

## Test Your Vocabulary • L-M (page 84)

1. languishing, feebly sentimental
2. a virulent or scurrilous satire, to write such
3. inert, spiritless, apathetic, dull, sluggish, faint, weak
4. a reading- or singing-desk in a church
5. away from or on the sheltered side of the wind
6. sleight of hand, conjuring tricks, jugglery
7. slowness, sluggishness
8. drowsiness or prolonged sleep, torpor, inertness, apathy
9. the writing or compilation of a dictionary
10. (of plants) like wood, woody
11. unfavorable place or condition of neglect, prison, oblivion
12. clear, pellucid, not turbid
13. ancestry, pedigree, lineal descent
14. supple, agile, lithesome
15. a metallic element
16. to go to law, contest, dispute
17. a gallery or arcade with one or more sides open to the air
18. talkative, wordy
19. a line on the earth cutting all meridians at same angle
20. clear, intelligible
21. mournful, doleful, dismal

22. crescent-shaped
23. vigorous, strong, lively
24. enjoy oneself, revel, indulge in luxury
25. to lay plots, intrigue, scheme
26. high-souled, above petty feelings or conduct
27. awkward, bungling, lacking in adroitness
28. doing harm or wrong, hurtful, crminal
29. a large tent
30. to grind with the teeth, chew
31. as sweet as honey
32. lying, untruthful, false
33. sprightly, volatile, ready-witted, of or containing mercury
34. showily attractive, befitting a harlot
35. over-careful about small details
36. threatening, menacing

## - DAY THIRTEEN -

### The Precise Word (page 86)

1. Marsupials
2. Flotsam
3. Origami
4. Palindrome
5. Jetsam
6. Griffin
7. Hyperbole
8. Sericulture
9. Cartomancy
10. Somniloquence
11. Amphibious
12. Bicentenary
13. Philately
14. Numismatics
15. Chameleon
16. Quiver
17. Pince-nez
18. Gargoyle
19. Fratricide
20. Tantony
21. Mnemonic
22. Honeycomb
23. Sextet
24. Ballistics

### Adjectives • 2 (page 87)

37. very small, trifling, detailed
38. that can be shaped by hammering, adaptable, pliable
39. leading a wandering life
40. relating to the sense of smell
41. sluggish, apathetic, not easily agitated
42. complaining, fretful, peevish
43. restless, uneasy, fidgety
44. impressionable, liable or sensitive to
45. dark, gloomy, dismal, melacholy
46. real, touchable, having substance
47. deputed, acting or done for another
48. truthful, speaking the truth
49. hard, laborious, strenuous, energetic
50. gentle, mild, kindly
51. convincing, compelling assent
52. rapid, superficial, hurried, hasty
53. respectful, showing deference
54. pleasing to the ear, free from harshness
55. limp, flabby, feeble, drooping
56. sticky, like glue, viscous
57. theatrical, stagy, acting a part
58. hasty, violent, acting with sudden energy
59. playful, waggish, full of jokes
60. languid, indifferent, unwilling to move
61. of sickly flavor, feebly or falsely sentimental
62. combative, warring, aggressively active
63. harmful, unwholesome, injurious
64. knowing all things
65. needless show of learning, undue attention to detail
66. abnormal, vast, enormous, marvellous
67. squeamish, easily upset or sickened

68. capable of feeling or sensation
69. very loud-voiced
70. perceptible to the touch, tangible
71. wordy, long-winded
72. temporal, earthly, mundane

### Complete the Word Challenge • N (page 88)

| | | |
|---|---|---|
| 1. Niggling | 9. Nocturnal | 17. Nonentity |
| 2. Notorious | 10. Nauseous | 18. Nihilism |
| 3. Noisome | 11. Niche | 19. Netsuke |
| 4. Nondescript | 12. Neolithic | 20. Nicotine |
| 5. Nutate | 13. Nectarine | 21. Neighborhood |
| 6. Natterjack | 14. Nodule | 22. Necessary |
| 7. Nitrogen | 15. Navigate | 23. Narcolepsy |
| 8. Neglect | 16. Nutriment | 24. Nadir |

### Test Your Vocabulary • M-N (page 89)

37. piece of bad luck, ill-luck, mishap
38. a hater of women
39. to alleviate, appease, moderate
40. to regulate, adjust, attune, vary tone of
41. giving warning, admonitory
42. caustic, biting, corrosive
43. at the point of death, dying
44. having great variety, many and various
45. splendidly generous, bountiful
46. a delicately-woven cotton fabric
47. to cut off, destroy, or render imperfect by removing limb or other part
48. countless, innumerable
49. unsophisticated, artless
50. self-love, self-admiration
51. the action or art of swimming
52. cloudy, hazy, vague, formless, like a nebula

53. art of prediction by communication with the dead, magic
54. wicked, iniquitous, villainous
55. to deny or nullify
56. that which can be disregarded or neglected
57. a new convert, novice, beginner
58. the study of clouds
59. ignorant of, agnostic
60. a bond, link, connection, connected group
61. to make a nest
62. stingy, sparing, miserly, mean, scanty
63. a list, set or system of names, terminology
64. lacking in warmth, enthusiasm or interest, indifferent
65. peerless, having no equal
66. home-sickeness or sentimental longing for the past
67. quack remedy, patent medicine, pet scheme for reform
68. speculative, imaginary, pertaining to a notion
69. like a stepmother
70. a slight variation or shade of meaning, feeling etc.
71. trifling, worthless, invalid, futile
72. to annul, cancel, make void

## - DAY FOURTEEN -
### Something in Commong (page 91)

1. Elements
2. Diseases
3. Old musical instruments
4. Dances
5. Clouds
6. Grammatical terms
7. Hats or head-gear
8. Boats
9. Winds
10. Carriages
11. Grassland plains
12. Parts of a castle
13. Vegetables
14. Tools
15. Wines
16. Furniture
17. Liqueurs
18. Explosives
19. Electrical units
20. Colors or pigments
21. Ball games
22. Dogs
23. Pieces of armor
24. Bridges

### Rare Words • 2 (page 92)

37. shamelessness, immodesty
38. increasing in warmth
39. ill constructed, crude, unpolished
40. flowing with milk
41. having broad leaves
42. shunning the light
43. one-eyed
44. given to much talking
45. surgical incision of the kidney
46. to declare a will orally
47. to darken, obscure, bewilder
48. forgetfulness
49. having five toes or fingers
50. pertaining to pigeons
51. feather-shaped
52. having several different names or titles
53. return to a youthful or flourishing state
54. a painter of mean or sordid subjects
55. a type of magic lantern
56. axe-shaped
57. having six eyes
58. the action of sneezing; a sneeze
59. an affliction of the eyes causing a squint
60. covered with stiff hairs
61. pertaining to household furniture; ornamental
62. wasting away
63. divination by means of ashes
64. darkness, obscurity
65. relating to transference of words, metaphorical; handed down or traditional

66. a combination of three vowel sounds in one syllable
67. to sting like a nettle
68. the murder of one's wife
69. relating to the evening; taking place in the evening
70. one who excercises delegated power; a deputy
71. to fly with a fluttering motion
72. the practice of fermentation

**You've already finished 14 days. Seven days to go!**

# DAY FIFTEEN

# FOREIGN WORDS AND PHRASES

What is the meaning of these words and phrases borrowed from foreign languages?

(Fr-French, It-Italian, L-Latin, G-German, Sp-Spanish)

1. A la carte (Fr)
2. Bête noire (Fr)
3. Bon mot (Fr)
4. Cognoscente (It)
5. Compos mentis (L)
6. Coup d'état (Fr)
7. De facto (L)
8. Esprit de corps (Fr)
9. Ex officio (L)
10. Fait accompli (Fr)
11. Hors de combat (Fr)
12. In situ (L)
13. Leitmotiv (G)
14. Mañana (Sp)
15. Olla podrida (Sp)
16. Par excellence (Fr)
17. Persona non grata (L)
18. Pièce de resistance (Fr)
19. Pied-à-terre (Fr)
20. Putsch (G)
21. Schadenfreude (G)
22. Sine die (L)
23. Sotto voce (It)
24. Tour de force (Fr)

## TEST YOUR VOCABULARY • O-P
Define the following words:

1. Obdurate
2. Obliterate
3. Oboe
4. Obsequious
5. Obstreperous
6. Ochlocracy
7. Officious
8. Oleaginous
9. Opaque
10. Opine
11. Opprobrium
12. Opulent
13. Orchestrate
14. Orifice
15. Ormolu
16. Orotund
17. Ossify
18. Ostensible
19. Ostentation
20. Ostracize
21. Otiose
22. Ovation
23. Overt
24. Ovoid
25. Palatable
26. Palpable
27. Paradigm
28. Parsimonious
29. Pellucid
30. Penurious
31. Peremptory
32. Perfunctory
33. Perspicacious
34. Pertinacious
35. Phrenetic
36. Pliable

## NAME THE CORRECT NOUN • 3

Name the noun that fits each of these definitions.

49. Art of clipping shrubs into ornamental shapes.
50. Long narrow sledge for downhill travel over prepared snow.
51. Alcoholic drink taken as an appetizer.
52. Malicious or wanton destruction by hostile agents.
53. Instrument for measuring atmospheric pressure.
54. Base-frame of a motor vehicle.
55. Set of seven voices or musical instruments.
56. Threadlike fiber or the wire in an electric bulb.
57. Man paid by a woman to be her escort or partner.
58. Hormone from the pancreas used to treat diabetes.
59. Open portico along front or side of a house.
60. The curved upper surface of liquid in a container.
61. Long pin for holding meat together while being cooked.
62. Old style of part-song for several voices.
63. Sweet fluid produced by plants and collected by bees.
64. Apparent displacement of an object caused by change of position of observer.
65. Lively second or third movement in a symphony or sonata.
66. Small container with mixed aromatic substances or perfumes.
67. Sheath that protects a sword or dagger.
68. Group of three related literary works.
69. The part of a monk's head left bare by shaving the hair.
70. Human being turned into a wolf.
71. Treatise for instruction in the Christian religion by question and answer.
72. Sleeping-room with a number of beds as in a monastery.

# DAY SIXTEEN

## LONG AND SHORT WORDS

Here are some extra-long words and then on the next page, some very short words. You may not know many of the long words, but you should know most of the short ones. Define the following words:

## LONG WORDS

1. Ambidextrous

2. Brachycephalic

3. Canaliculate

4. Commiseration

5. Condominium

6. Equiponderant

7. Flocci-nauci-nihili-
   pili-fication

8. Fore-topgallant

9. Funambulist

10. Impalpability

11. Indefatigable

12. Isoperimetrical

13. Lepidopterist

14. Malacodermatous

15. Octingentenary

16. Parallelepiped

17. Premonstratensian

18. Rendezvous

19. Sanguification

20. Sesquipedalian

21. Tergiversation

22. Testudinarious

23. Ultracrepidarian

24. Valetudinarian

## SHORT WORDS

25. Acrid
26. Aft
27. Aloof
28. Banal
29. Crypt
30. Doggo
31. Eke
32. Fez
33. Flair
34. Fop
35. Glut
36. Haply

37. Ingot
38. Mete
39. Muggy
40. Numb
41. Opal
42. Pawky
43. Rabid
44. Rant
45. Salvo
46. Tryst
47. Vapid
48. Vial

## UNUSUAL WORDS WITH AN "H"

Define this collection of odd words beginning with "H".

49. Hab-nab
50. Handy-dandy
51. Hanky-panky
52. Harum-scarum
53. Heebie-jeebies
54. Helter-skelter
55. Hiccius doccius
56. Higgledy-piggledy
57. Hitty-missy
58. Hob-nob
59. Hocus-pocus
60. Hoddy-doddy

61. Hogen Mogen
62. Hoi polloi
63. Hoity-toity
64. Holus-bolus
65. Hotchpotch
66. Hot-pot
67. Hubble-bubble
68. Hugger-mugger
69. Humdrum
70. Humpty-dumpty
71. Hurdy-gurdy
72. Hurly-burly

## COMPLETE THE WORD CHALLENGE • O

Complete the following words from the given meanings.

1. O _ _ _ _ _ s  a type of vehicle
2. O _ _ r _ _ s  burdensome
3. O _ _ _ c _ _ n  a maker of spectacles
4. O _ _ o _ _ n  a type of seat
5. O _ l _ _ _ t _ _ y  legally or morally binding
6. O _ _ r _ g _ _ _ s  immoderate, extravagant
7. O _ r _ r _  a model of the planetary system
8. O _ _ _ l _ _ t _  to swing like a pendulum, vacillate
9. O _ n _ x _ o _ _  offensive, objectionable
10. O _ u _ _ _ t  an eye-specialist
11. O _ _ l _ s _  a tall stone monument
12. O _ _ n _ _ s  inauspicious, threatening
13. O _ v _ _ t _  to get round, prevent
14. O _ _ or _ _ n _  favorable, well-timed
15. O _ s _ _ _ t _  disused, antiquated
16. O _ n _ _ e  elaborately decorated or adorned
17. Ob _ i _ i _ _ _  forgetful, unmindful of
18. O _ t _ m _ _  the best or most favorable
19. O _ t _ _ d _ _  conventional, correct
20. O _ _ _ _ n  a gas essential to life
21. O _ c _ _ r _ _ c _  a happening or incident
22. O _ _ _ _ e _ a _ _ _ n  a person eighty years old
23. O _ t _ _ e  blunt, dull, stupid
24. O _ st _ c _ _  a hindrance or impediment

# DAY SEVENTEEN

## CONFUSING WORDS QUIZ

There are many words that are often confused with other somewhat similar words. Can you explain the difference between the two words in each pair?

1. Continual     and     Continuous
2. Alternate             Alternative
3. Practical             Practicable
4. Decompose             Discompose
5. Cryptogam             Cryptogram
6. Gourmand              Gourmet
7. Deprecate             Depreciate
8. Exceptional           Exceptionable
9. Luxuriant             Luxurious
10. Mendacity            Mendicity
11. Desiccate            Desecrate
12. Elicit               Illicit
13. Titillate            Titivate
14. Turbid               Turgid
15. Venal                Venial
16. Inflammable          Inflammatory
17. Tractable            Tractile
18. Ingenious            Ingenuous
19. Abrogate             Arrogate
20. Adhere               Cohere
21. Credible             Creditable
22. Equable              Equitable
23. Contemptible         Contemptuous
24. Deduce               Deduct

## COMPLETE THE WORD CHALLENGE • P

Complete the following words from the given meanings.

1. P _ _ d _ _ _ m _ _ t  an unpleasant or dangerous situation
2. P _ _ v _ _ _ n _  having foresight, thrifty
3. P _ _ n _ c _ _ _ s  quarrelsome, given to fighting
4. P _ o _ _ r _ _ e  lying face downwards on the ground
5. P _ r _ _ c _ _ _ s  destructive, ruinous
6. P _ _ s _ g _  to portend, give warning of
7. P _ t _ l _ _ t  peevishly impatient, irritable
8. P _ _ t _ t _ _ _  a commonplace remark
9. P _ _ d _ _ _ l  wasteful, lavish
10. P _ _ d _ _ o _ _ u _  uproar, confusion
11. P _ o _ _ f _ _  abundantly productive of
12. P _ _ t _ _ _ t _ _ _  type of leather trunk
13. P _ n _ _ _ n _  repentant, contrite
14. P _ r _ _ r _ t _  to make holes in, pierce
15. P _ _ m _ _ _ _ t  supreme, pre-eminent
16. P _ _ p _ _ t _ _ o _ _  absurd, ridiculous
17. P _ t _ _ t _ t _  a monarch or ruler
18. P _ _ g _ _ n _  sharp, pungent
19. P _ r _ x _ s _  a fit of rage or laughter
20. Pr _ _ _ nt _ _ _ s  ostentatious, claiming great merit
21. P _ _ _ p _ _ _ y  boundary line or surface
22. P _ u _ _ _ t  discreet, judicious
23. P _ _ m _ n _ _ _  connected with the lungs
24. P _ _ _ _ d  decomposed, rotten

# TEST YOUR VOCABULARY • P-R

### Define the following words:

37. Ponderous

38. Pragmatism

39. Precocious

40. Predilection

41. Premeditated

42. Presentiment

43. Prestidigitation

44. Prevaricate

45. Procrastinate

46. Promulgate

47. Punctilious

48. Pusillanimous

49. Ramify

50. Rancor

51. Rapacious

52. Ratiocinate

53. Recalcitrant

54. Recollect

55. Recondite

56. Recrudesce

57. Redolent

58. Refulgent

59. Remonstrate

60. Reprehend

61. Rescind

62. Resuscitate

63. Reticulate

64. Rhabdomancy

65. Rigmarole

66. Risible

67. Rococo

68. Rotund

69. Rubicund

70. Rubiginous

71. Rumbustious

72. Ruse

# DAY EIGHTEEN

## HOMONYM CHALLENGE

There are many words which, though spelled the same, have two or more quite different meanings; they are known as homonyms. Can you supply the word which fits these definitions?

1. to find fault; a species of fish
2. a species of tree; a carpenter's tool
3. a small sum or amount; a sweet confection
4. a mail-boat; a small parcel
5. a species of mammal; a stamp or impression of authenticity
6. a period of the year; to mature or ripen
7. the capital funds of a company; a flower
8. a receptacle; a species of tree
9. relating to the body; a military rank
10. a forest-tree; the residue of burning
11. a current of air; a preliminary sketch or plan
12. a recurring verse in song; to abstain or forbear
13. a garment; a headland
14. a sharp reply; a vessel for heating liquids
15. part of a ship; a card-game
16. a large bird; a machine for raising things
17. useless odds-and-ends; to move heavily
18. a narrow pass; to corrupt or befoul
19. a species of fish; a deep voice or sound
20. kind of beer; a gate-keeper
21. an obsolete weapon; a species of fish
22. a tiresome talkative person; a tidal-wave
23. a tool; a military exercise
24. a measure; a fish's organ

## COMPLETE THE WORD CHALLENGE• R

Complete the following words from the given meanings.

1. Re _ _ m _ _ _ t  lying down, reclining
2. R _ _ _ c _ _ e  the killing of a king
3. R _ p _ r _ _ e  a witty reply or retort
4. R _ m _ _ e _ _ t _  to reward or pay for services
5. R _ _ r _ m _ n _  to rebuke, reprove, censure
6. R _ _ l _ _ a  a duplicate or facsimile
7. R _ _ s _ _ c _ l _  rickety, tumble-down
8. R _ s _ n _ _ t  re-echoing, resounding
9. R _ tr _ _ _ o _ r  part of a cathedral or church
10. R _ f _ _ c _ _ _ y  stubborn, rebellious
11. R _ s _ _ u _  remainder, rest
12. R _ s _ l _ _ d _ _ t  shining, brilliant
13. R _ u _ _ us  hoarse, harsh-sounding
14. R _ _ t _ _ m  a platform for public speakers
15. R _ _ i _ _ l _ _ _  absurd, laughable
16. R _ d _ _ d _ n _  superfluous, excessive
17. R _ _ d _ d _ _ d _ _ _  a type of evergreen shrub
18. R _ s _ _ _ t _  determined, unshrinking
19. R _ c _ p _ _ c _ _  inversely correspondent, complement-
    ary
20. R _ v _ r _ _ r _ _ _  to re-echo, reflect, return
21. R _ v _ _ o _ _  famished, hungry
22. R _ _ _ l _ _ _ n  armed resistance, revolt
23. R _ _ _ v _ _ _ t _  to make young again
24. R _ c _ p _ _ _ t _  to restore, recover from illness

## TEST YOUR VOCABULARY • S-T
Define the following words:

1. Salubrious
2. Sarcophagus
3. Scintillate
4. Scurrilous
5. Sedulous
6. Senescent
7. Sententious
8. Serendipity
9. Sibilant
10. Simulacrum
11. Smithereens
12. Solicitous
13. Somnolent
14. Sonorous
15. Soupçon
16. Specious
17. Sporadic
18. Strategem
19. Strident
20. Suave
21. Sullen
22. Sultry
23. Sumptuous
24. Surreptitious
25. Taciturn
26. Talisman
27. Tarantella
28. Tarantula
29. Tawdry
30. Temerity
31. Tendentious
32. Tenuous
33. Thaumaturge
34. Thrall
35. Timorous
36. Tintinnabulation

# CHEMISTRY, MATH AND PHYSICS

Define the following words, all of which you may come across in the course of normal reading.

| | |
|---|---|
| 1. Asteroid | 13. Methane |
| 2. Atmospherics | 14. Micron |
| 3. Barbiturate | 15. Myopia |
| 4. Bronze | 16. Ozone |
| 5. Casein | 17. Polaroid |
| 6. Cathode | 18. Polygon |
| 7. Erg | 19. Refraction |
| 8. Fluoridation | 20. Specific gravity |
| 9. Halogen | 21. Spectroscope |
| 10. Integer | 22. Surd |
| 11. Isosceles | 23. Tangent |
| 12. Light-year | 24. Torque |

# DAY NINETEEN

# EPONYMOUS WORDS

Words derived from the names of people are knows as eponymous words. Name the words that fit these definitions.

1. Coat waterproofed with rubber or other material.
2. Instrument with knife-blade for beheading people.
3. Sofa with padded back and sides.
4. Slices of bread with meat, cheese, jam, etc. between.
5. Rigid or strict disciplinarian.
6. Portrait profile in black outline.
7. Waterproof rubber boot reaching the knee.
8. Make a road with layers of broken stone.
9. Horse-drawn cab for two with driver behind.
10. Writing for the blind with embossed letters.
11. Knitted jacket or over-waistcoat.
12. Refuse social or commericial relations because of political or other differences.
13. Woman's loose knee-length undergarments.
14. Expurgate book by omitting indelicate words.
15. Fragments of metal scattered from exploding projectile.
16. Crane or hoisting-machine, framework over oil-well.
17. Unit of electrical current.
18. Practice of inducing hypnotic state in a patient.
19. A cross between a raspberry and a blackberry.
20. Deceitful, cunning, scheming, unscrupulous.
21. Unit of electrical resistance.
22. Railway carriage designed as saloon or sleeping-car.
23. One who gets pleasure from cruelty to others
24. Brass wind instrument with clarinet mouthpiece.

# TEST YOUR VOCABULARY • T-U-V
### Define the following words:

| | |
|---|---|
| 37. Torpid | 55. Vehement |
| 38. Tortuous | 56. Verbatim |
| 39. Toxophily | 57. Verisimilitude |
| 40. Traduce | 58. Vermicular |
| 41. Transmute | 59. Vespiary |
| 42. Tremulous | 60. Vicarage |
| 43. Trenchant | 61. Vicinity |
| 44. Tribulation | 62. Virile |
| 45. Truculent | 63. Virulent |
| 46. Tumid | 64. Viscous |
| 47. Tutelage | 65. Vituperate |
| 48. Typography | 66. Volatile |
| 49. Ubiquitous | 67. Voracious |
| 50. Umbrage | 68. Vouchsafe |
| 51. Unkempt | 69. Waive |
| 52. Uxorious | 70. Whimsical |
| 53. Vacillate | 71. Whittle |
| 54. Vacuous | 72. Wreckage |

## COMPLETE THE WORD CHALLENGE • S

Complete the following words from the given meanings.

1. Se _ _ _ h _ _ e  a type of signalling apparatus
2. S _ _ g _ _ s _  inactive, torpid, indolent
3. S _ p _ _ _ f _ _  tending to produce sleep
4. S _ n _ _ s _ _  a summary or conspectus
5. S _ n _ _ _ s  tortuous, undulating
6. S _ _ _ l _ _ r _ l  funereal, dismal
7. S _ c _ _ h _ _ t  a flatterer or toady
8. S _ _ d _ n _ _  bitter, scornful, cynical
9. S _ b _ _ _ t  to disturb or overthrow
10. S _ r _ _ _ _ d  having a saw-like edge
11. S _ g _ _ g _ _ _  to set apart, separate
12. S _ _ _ c _ _ _ n _  a deadly poison
13. S _ _ m _ _ _  power of resistance or endurance
14. S _ c _ _ s _ _ c _  inviolable, sacred
15. So _ _ c _ _ m  a grammatical error
16. S _ r _ n _ _ n _  strict, rigorous
17. Sc _ _ _ _ l _ _ s  careful, conscientious
18. St _ _ n _ _ _  motionless, dull
19. S _ r _ o _ _ _ l  relating to the art of tailoring
20. S _ u _ _ n _ _ u _  amazing, astounding
21. S _ _ p _ _ _ t _  to demand or insist upon as a condition
22. S _ _ v _ _ _ r _  a docker
23. S _ _ _ t _ _  a ghost
24. S _ _ c _ _ y  to name or mention expressly

# DAY TWENTY

## "ISMS"

The words which fit the following definitions all end in *"ism"*. How many do you know?

1. A new word or expression, or the use of new words.
2. A ridiculous misuse of a word, usually for one resembling it.
3. The transposition of the beginnings of two adjacent words.
4. The use of another person's thoughts or writings as one's own.
5. A mild expression used as a substitute for a blunt one.
6. Artificial or affected style of writing.
7. The art style which presents objects as geometrical shapes.
8. Denial of the existence of a God.
9. Belief that the existence of God cannot be known or proved.
10. Doctrine that all is God and God is all.
11. Belief in God without proof or revelation.
12. Sleep-walking.
13. Perversion in which sufferer derives pleasure from pain.
14. Belief that everything that happens is predetermined by fate.
15. An expression belonging to ordinary conversation or common speech.
16. A principle expressed concisely, a maxim.
17. Conduct expressing patient endurance and repression of feelings.
18. The action of passing judgement upon anything; fault-finding
19. Artificially producing a state of deep sleep.
20. Religious rite of initiation into the Church.
21. Regard for others as a principle of action.
22. Exaggerated and warlike patriotism
23. An old or obsolete word or expression.
24. Art form which represents the phenomena of dreams and the subconscious.

## COMPLETE THE WORD CHALLENGE • T

Complete the following words from the given meanings.

1. T _ m _ _ s _ _ _ _ s  stormy, violent
2. T _ _ n _ _ _ n _  impermanent, momentary
3. T _ _ b _ _ _ n _  disturbed, tumultuous
4. To _ _ r _ _ _  to endure or permit
5. T _ r _ _ _ l  agitation, trouble
6. T _ _ s _ s  a dissertation, exercise
7. T _ _ _ _ _ t  a three-pronged weapon
8. T _ _ n _ _ _ t  part of a church
9. T _ n _ _ _ _ z _  to torment or tease
10. T _ _ g _ _ d _ _ e  a cave-dweller
11. T _ _ t _ t _ _ _  experimental
12. T _ _ _ _ m  a self-evident truth
13. T _ _ _ d _ _ _ y  the art of stuffing and mounting animal skins
14. T _ _ _ s _ _ a _  a bride's outfit
15. T _ _ v _ _ t _  a ridiculous imitation
16. T _ a _ _ u _ _  calm, serene
17. T _ _ p _ _ l _ _  a type of waterproof cloth
18. T _ n _ _ r _ _ l  relating to a barber
19. T _ r _ _ e  a long speech of denunciation
20. T _ a _ _ c _ _ _ y  the path of a projectile through the air
21. T _ _ _ f _ _  frugal, economical
22. T _ r _ _ t _ _ _  a tract of land, a region
23. T _ _ _ d  lukewarm
24. T _ n _ _ i _ _ s  holding fast, resolute

# DAY TWENTY-ONE

## COMPLETE THE WORD CHALLENGE • U-W

Complete the following words from the given meanings.

1. V _ v _ c _ _ _ s   lively, animated
2. U _ d _ _ _ t _ _ n   rising and falling like waves
3. U _ _ l _ _ _   usefulness
4. Va _ _ _ i _ _   a holiday
5. V _ _ t _ g _   giddiness, dizziness
6. V _ l _ _   courage, prowess
7. V _ _ n _ _ _ _ l _   susceptible of injury, open to attack
8. V _ n _ _ i _ _   to conquer or overcome
9. U _ b _ _ _   courteous, suave, refined
10. V _ r _ i _ i _ _   a color
11. W _ _ m _ _ _   a soft cry or whine
12. Va _ a _ _ n _   a wanderer or vagrant
13. V _ _ _ f _ r _ _   noisy, clamorous
14. U _ _ n _ _ _ _ s   all of one mind, agreeing
15. V _ n _ _ _ t _   to regard with respect, revere
16. W _ _ t _ _   to twist or squirm
17. Vi _ i _ _ n _ _   watchfulness, caution
18. V _ _ _ i _ u _ _   a hall or lobby
19. V _ r _ _ c _ _ _ r   native, indigenous
20. W _ _ _ e _ n _ _ _   desert, uninhabited area
21. W _ _ s _ _ e   charming, engaging
22. V _ n _ _ c _ _ v _   revengeful
23. Wi _ _ n _ _   shrivelled, dried up
24. V _ _ u _ _ _ _ n   estimation of worth

## FOUR-LETTER WORDS

Define the following four-letter words (polite ones!)

| | |
|---|---|
| 1. Adit | 13. Hint |
| 2. Agog | 14. Icon |
| 3. Avid | 15. Ilex |
| 4. Awry | 16. Iota |
| 5. Bode | 17. Jamb |
| 6. Cede | 18. Kink |
| 7. Coma | 19. Lyre |
| 8. Crux | 20. Mien |
| 9. Dank | 21. Mire |
| 10. Deft | 22. Oast |
| 11. Gist | 23. Rife |
| 12. Glib | 24. Tome |

## LATIN PHRASES

Define these common Latin phrases.

| | |
|---|---|
| 1. Bona fide | 13. Ultimo |
| 2. Ad lib | 14. Per annum |
| 3. Sine qua non | 15. A fortiori |
| 4. Ad infinitum | 16. Caveat emptor |
| 5. Terra firma | 17. Infra dig |
| 6. Status quo | 18. Ipso facto |
| 7. Pro tem | 19. Ultra vires |
| 8. Non sequitur | 20. Vice versa |
| 9. Tempus fugit | 21. Sub judice |
| 10. Pro rata | 22. In camera |
| 11. Quid pro quo | 23. Per se |
| 12. In toto | 24. Ex officio |

# WEEK THREE

## - DAY FIFTEEN -

### Foreign Words and Phrases (page 113)

1. ordered as separate items from the menu
2. person or thing particularly disliked
3. witty saying
4. connoisseur
5. in ones' right mind
6. sudden or violent change of government
7. in actual fact or reality
8. loyalty to a body by its members
9. by virtue of one's office
10. thing done and past arguing against
11. out of the fight, disabled
12. in its original place
13. theme, in a piece of music or work, associated with a person, idea or sentiment
14. tomorrow, indefinite future
15. mixture, mish-mash
16. above all others that may be so called, pre-eminently
17. person not acceptable to certain others
18. the most important or remarkable item
19. occasional residence or temporary quarters
20. attempt at revolution
21. malicious enjoyment of others' misfortunes
22. with no appointed date
23. in an undertone
24. feat of strength or skill

## Test Your Vocabulary • O-P (page 114)

1. hardened in evil, unyielding, stubborn
2. to erase, efface, blot out, delete
3. a musical instrument
4. servile, fawning, sycophantic
5. noisy, vociferous, unruly
6. government by mob-rule
7. doing more than required, meddlesome
8. having properties of oil, producing oil, oily, greasy
9. not transmitting light, not transparent, obscure
10. to hold or express an opinion
11. disgrace, infamy, reproach
12. rich, wealthy
13. to compose or arrange for an orchestra
14. an aperture, vent, or perforation
15. gilded bronze, gold-colored alloy of copper, zinc and tin
16. imposing or dignified way of speaking, inflated, pompous
17. to turn into bone, to harden
18. professed, pretended, put forth as genuine
19. pretentious display, showing-off
20. to banish, expel, exclude from society etc.
21. superfluous, useless, sterile
22. enthusiastic applause
23. open to view, evident, unconcealed
24. like an egg, egg-shaped
25. pleasant to the taste, savory
26. tangible, readily perceived, apparent, obvious
27. an example, pattern
28. careful with money, sparing
29. transparent, clear
30. poor, needy, grudging
31. dogmatic, imperious, intolerant, dictatorial

32. done as routine or without interest, superficial
33. having mental penetration or discernment
34. persistent, stubborn, obstinate
35. frantic, fanatic
36. flexible, supple, yielding

### Name the Correct Noun • 3 (page 115)

49. Topiary
50. Toboggan
51. Aperitif
52. Sabotage
53. Barometer
54. Chassis
55. Septet
56. Filament

57. Gigolo
58. Insulin
59. Veranda
60. Meniscus
61. Skewer
62. Madrigal
63. Nectar
64. Parallax

65. Scherzo
66. Pomander
67. Scabbard
68. Trilogy
69. Tonsure
70. Werewolf
71. Catechism
72. Dormitory

## - DAY SIXTEEN -

### Long Words (page 117)

1. being able to use both hands equally well
2. short-headed, short-skulled
3. having a longitudinal groove or minute channel
4. pity or sorrow for another person's distress
5. joint control of a state's affairs by other states
6. of equal weight, evenly balanced
7. the action of estimating as worthless
8. the mast above the fore-topmast of a ship
9. a rope-walker or rope-dancer
10. the quality of being imperceptible to the touch or intangible
11. incapable of being tired out or wearied, unremitting
12. having equal perimeters
13. a person who studies butterflies and moths
14. having a soft skin (of animals)
15. the eight-hundredth anniversary of an event
16. a solid figure contained by six parallelograms
17. an order of regular canons
18. an appointed place of meeting
19. the formation of blood, conversion into blood
20. a word of many syllables, given to long words
21. the forsaking or deserting of a cause or party
22. of the character of a tortoise
23. going beyond one's province or knowledge
24. a person in poor health, especially one concerned with his own ailments

### Short Words (page 117)

25. bitter, pungent, corrosive, irritating
26. near or towards the stern
27. at a distance from, apart

28. commonplace, trite, trivial
29. an underground chamber or vault, especially beneath a church
30. to lie quiet or hidden
31. to increase, add to, supplement
32. a Turkish skull-cap in the form of a cone
33. discernment, instinct for what is excellent
34. a dandy, a vain man
35. a surfeit of a commodity; to feed or fill to excess
36. by chance or accident; perhaps
37. a mass of cast metal, especially of gold, silver or steel
38. to measure, deal out, allot
39. damp, close and warm, stifling
40. deprived of feeling, helpless
41. a type of gemstone
42. artful, sly, cunning, shrewd
43. furious, violent, unreasoning
44. to speak bombastically or loudly; empty talk or tirade
45. a salute by artillery guns; a reservation or saving clause
46. an agreement to meet at a certain place and time
47. flat, dull, insipid, lifeless
48. a small vessel for holding liquids

### Odd Words With an H (page 118)

49. get or lose , hit or miss, anyhow
50. a children's game in which an object is concealed in the hand
51. jugglery, trickery, double dealing
52. reckless, wild, rash
53. a dance resembling the blues, also the blues
54. in disorderly haste; pell-mell; a large slide in a fair ground
55. magic words or formula used by jugglers
56. confusion or disorderly jumble
57. hit or miss, random, haphazard

58. to drink together, be on familiar terms with
59. jugglery, trickery, deception
60. short and dumpy, a snail (dialect)
61. a contemptuous word for the Dutch (formerly the high and mighty)
62. the masses, the rabble
63. frolicsome, petulant, flighty
64. all in a hump, all at one
65. a mixture, medley, jumble
66. a dish of meat and potatoes cooked in a pot
67. a type of Eastern smoking-pipe; also confused talk
68. disorderly, confused; also secret, clandestine
69. commonplace, monotonous, dull
70. a short, dumpy person
71. a musical instrument played by turning a handle; also name given to the barrel-organ
72. commotion, uproar, confusion

### Complete the Word Challenge • O (page 119)

1. Omnibus
2. Onerous
3. Optician
4. Ottoman
5. Obligatory
6. Outrageous
7. Orrery
8. Oscillate
9. Obnoxious
10. Oculist
11. Obelisk
12. Ominous
13. Obviate
14. Opportune
15. Obsolete
16. Ornate
17. Oblivious
18. Optimum
19. Orthodox
20. Oxygen
21. Occurrence
22. Octogenarian
23. Obtuse
24. Obstacle

## - DAY SEVENTEEN -

### Confusing Words Quiz (page 121)

1. Continual = always going on, perpetual, incessant, never coming to an end. Continuous = unbroken from start to finish, uninterrupted in time or sequence.

2. Alternate = by turns, i.e. two things succeeding each other in turn, one after the other. Alternative = the choice of one of two things or courses of action.

3. Practical = of or relating to the practice of something as opposed to the theory. Practicable = capable of being carried out or accomplished, feasible.

4. Decompose = to separate into constituent parts or elements, to decay or rot. Discompose = to disturb the composure or calmness of, to agitate or ruffle.

5. Cryptogam = a species of plant with no stamens and pistils and no flowers. Cryptogram = something in cypher or code.

6. Gourmand = a judge or lover of good eating. Gourmet = a connoisseur of good food, delicacies and wine.

7. Deprecate = to plead or pray against something, to express disapproval of. Depreciate = to diminish in value, to disparage or belittle.

8. Exceptional = forming an exception, out of the ordinary, unusual. Exceptionable = open to exception or objection.

9. Luxuriant = growing profusely, exuberant, prolific, rich, producing abundantly. Luxurious = given to luxury or self-indulgence.

10. Mendacity = untruthfulness, habitual lying or deceiving. Mendicity = the practice of begging, the condition of a beggar.

11. Desiccate = to make dry, or dry up for preservation. Desecrate = to commit outrage on or profane something sacred.

12. Elicit = to draw forth, to draw out information, to evoke a response. Illicit = unlawful, forbidden, not allowed by law, rule or custom.
13. Titillate = to excite or stimulate the mind or senses, to tickle. Titivate = to make oneself more attractive by small additions to one's toilet, to put the finishing touches to some thing.
14. Turbid = not clear, cloudy, muddy, mentally confused or muddled. Turgid = swollen, distended, inflated.
15. Venal = of persons capable of being bought over, of a mercenary character, of offices etc. capable of being acquired by purchase. Venial = not grave, trivial, worthy of pardon or forgiveness.
16. Inflammable = capable of being inflamed, easily set on fire (strangely enough "flammable" means exactly the same). Inflammatory = tending to excite passion or anger, to inflame the blood, to stimulate.
17. Tractable = easily managed, docile, compliant. Tractile = that which can be drawn, e.g. money from a bank.
18. Ingenious = showing cleverness of invention or construction. Ingenuous = straightforward, open, candid, frank, artless.
19. Abrogate = to repeal or do away with. Arrogate = to claim that which one is not entitled to, to appropriate without reason, to assume without foundation.
20. Adhere = to stick fast to something, to cleave to a person or party. Cohere = to stick together, to be united in action.
21. Credible = capable of being believed. Creditable = that which brings credit or honor, reputable.
22. Equable = uniform, free from inequalities or variation. Equitable = characterized by fairness and impartiality.
23. Contemptible = worthy of contempt, despicable. Contemptuous = showing contempt, disdainful, scornful.

24. Deduce = to draw as a conclusion from something known or assumed, to derive by reasoning, to infer. Deduct = to take away or subtract from a sum or amount.

### Complete the Word Challenge • P (page 122)

| | | |
|---|---|---|
| 1. Predicament | 9. Prodigal | 17. Potentate |
| 2. Provident | 10. Pandemonium | 18. Poignant |
| 3. Pugnacious | 11. Prolific | 19. Paroxysm |
| 4. Prostrate | 12. Portmanteau | 20. Pretentious |
| 5. Pernicious | 13. Penitent | 21. Periphery |
| 6. Presage | 14. Perforate | 22. Prudent |
| 7. Petulant | 15. Prominent | 23. Pulmonary |
| 8. Platitude | 16. Preposterous | 24. Putrid |

### Test Your Vocabulary • P-R (page 123)

37. heavy, massive, unwieldy, laborious
38. pedantry, matter-of-fact treatment, a philosophical doctrine
39. prematurely developed, fruiting early
40. a mental preference, partiality
41. previously planned, thought out beforehand
42. foreboding, vague expectation
43. sleight of hand, conjuring
44. to speak or act evasively, equivocate
45. to defer, delay
46. to make known, proclaim
47. attentive to or observant of nice points of behaviour
48. faint-hearted, cowardly, mean-spirited
49. to form branches, branch out, spread like branches
50. bitter ill-feeling, malignant hatred, spitefulness
51. grasping, greedy, predatory
52. to reason
53. disobedient, refractory
54. to recall to mind, remember
55. abstruse, obscure, profound

56. to break out again
57. smelling of, full of the smell or scent of
58. shining brilliantly, radiant
59. to protest against, expostulate
60. to rebuke, censure, find fault with
61. to annul, revoke, repeal
62. to restore to life or revive
63. to divide or be divided into a network
64. divining by use of a rod, especially for water
65. rambling or meaningless talk, incoherent
66. inclined to laughter, relating to laughter
67. a highly-ornate style of eighteenth-century art
68. (of speech) sonorous, (of persons) rounded, plump
69. ruddy, reddish, red-faced
70. rusty, rust-colored
71. boisterous, uproarious
72. a trick or stratagem

## - DAY EIGHTEEN -

### Homonym Challenge (page 125)

| | | |
|---|---|---|
| 1. Carp | 9. Corporal | 17. Lumber |
| 2. Plane | 10. Ash | 18. Defile |
| 3. Trifle | 11. Draught | 19. Bass |
| 4. Packet | 12. Refrain | 20. Porter |
| 5. Seal | 13. Cape | 21. Pike |
| 6. Season | 14. Retort | 22. Bore |
| 7. Stock | 15. Bridge | 23. Drill |
| 8. Box | 16. Crane | 24. Gill |

## Complete the Word Challenge • R (page 126)

| | | |
|---|---|---|
| 1. Recumbent | 9. Retrochoir | 17. Rhododendron |
| 2. Regicide | 10. Refractory | 18. Resolute |
| 3. Repartee | 11. Residue | 19. Reciprocal |
| 4. Remunerate | 12. Resplendent | 20. Reverberate |
| 5. Reprimand | 13. Raucous | 21. Ravenous |
| 6. Replica | 14. Rostrum | 22. Rebellion |
| 7. Ramshackle | 15. Ridiculous | 23. Rejuvenate |
| 8. Resonant | 16. Redundant | 24. Recuperate |

## Test Your Vocabulary • S-T (page 127)

1. favorable to health, healthy
2. a stone coffin
3. to sparkle, twinkle, emit sparks
4. coarseness of language, grossly abusive
5. diligent, persistent, assiduous
6. growing old, elderly
7. aphoristic, affectedly formal, given to moralizing
8. the knack of making happy discoveries by accident
9. having or making a hissing sound
10. an image, imitation or likeness of something
11. small fragments
12. anxious, eager, troubled, concerned
13. sleepy, drowsy
14. loud-sounding, resonant, having a full voice
15. a very small quantity or dash of something
16. apparently attractive or plausible but not genuine or sincere
17. occurring here and there, scattered, isolated
18. an artifice or trick
19. loud and harsh, shrill
20. pleasing, agreeable, soothing, blandly polite
21. ill-humored, morose, unsociable, dismal
22. oppressively hot

23. costly and magnificent
24. secret, clandestine, stealthy
25. reserved in speech, not given to talking
26. a charm, amulet
27. a South Italian dance
28. a large spider
29. cheap finery, showy but worthless
30. rashness, recklessness
31. having an underlying purpose, or a purposed tendency
32. thin, slender, unsubstantial
33. a worker of miracles, wonder-worker
34. a serf or slave, bondage, servitude, enslaved
35. timid, full of fear
36. bell-ringing, the tinkling of bells

### Chemistry, Math and Physics (page 128)

1. a small planet orbiting round the sun
2. electrical discharges in the atmosphere
3. a drug made from barbituric acid, given to promote sleep
4. an alloy of copper and tin
5. the protein found in milk (cheese is mainly casein)
6. a negative electrical plate or electrode
7. a unit of work or energy
8. the adding of fluoride to drinking water
9. any one of these four elements: fluorine, iodine, bromine, chlorine
10. any whole number e.g. 15, 6, 100 (not e.g. 3 1/2)
11. a triangle with two sides or two angles equal
12. the distance travelled by light in one year
13. a compound of hydrogen and carbon, also called marsh gas or fire-damp
14. a thousandth part of a millimeter
15. short-sightedness

## - DAY NINETEEN -

### Eponymous Words (page 130)

1. Macintosh
2. Guillotine
3. Chesterfield
4. Sandwich
5. Martinet
6. Silhouette
7. Wellington
8. Macadamize
9. Hansom
10. Braille
11. Cardigan
12. Boycott
13. Bloomers
14. Bowdlerize
15. Shrapnel
16. Derrick
17. Ampere
18. Mesmerism
19. Loganberry
20. Machiavellian
21. Ohm
22. Pullman
23. Sadist
24. Saxophone

### Test Your Vocabulary • T-W (page 131)

37. numb, dormant, sluggish, apathetic
38. full of twists, winding, crooked, devious
39. the practice of archery
40. to misrepresent, defame, slander
41. to change the form or nature of, convert, alter
42. trembling, quivering, fearful
43. incisive, clear-cut, decisive
44. severe suffering or affliction, oppression
45. fierce, cruel, ferocious, scathing, savage
46. swollen, inflated, protuberant
47. guardianship, tuition, under protection
48. the art of printing, the arrangement of printed matter
49. everywhere present, widely distributed
50. resentment, offence, sense of slight
51. untidy, of neglected appearance
52. excessively devoted to one's wife
53. to waver, oscillate, sway from side to side
54. empty, void, expressionless
55. violent, intense, ardent, with great force or strength

56. word for word
57. the appearance or semblace of being true
58. worm-like, wavy
59. a wasps' nest
60. the benefice or residence of a vicar
61. nearness to, surrounding district
62. manly, full of masculine strength
63. poisonous, malignant
64. like glue, sticky, not fluid
65. to abuse, revile
66. changeable, transient, readily vanishing or evaporating
67. greedy, ravenous
68. condescend to do or give something
69. to forgo or relinquish a right or claim
70. capricious, fantastic, full of whims
71. to slice or shave with a knife, to wear away or reduce
72. remnants of a wrecked vessel, house etc.

### Complete the Word Challenge • S (page132)

| | | |
|---|---|---|
| 1. Semaphore | 9. Subvert | 17. Scrupulous |
| 2. Sluggish | 10. Serrated | 18. Stagnant |
| 3. Soporific | 11. Segregate | 19. Sartorial |
| 4. Synopsis | 12. Strychnine | 20. Stupendous |
| 5. Sinuous | 13. Stamina | 21. Stipulate |
| 6. Sepulchral | 14. Sacrosanct | 22. Stevedore |
| 7. Sycophant | 15. Solecism | 23. Spectre |
| 8. Sardonic | 16. Stringent | 24. Specify |

## - DAY TWENTY -

### "-Isms" (page 134)

1. Neologism
2. Malapropism
3. Spoonerism
4. Plagiarism
5. Euphemism
6. Euphuism
7. Cubism
8. Atheism
9. Agnosticism
10. Pantheism
11. Deism
12. Somnambulism
13. Masochism
14. Fatalism
15. Colloquialism
16. Aphorism
17. Stoicism
18. Criticism
19. Hypnotism
20. Baptism
21. Altruism
22. Chauvinism
23. Archaism
24. Surrealism

### Complete the Word Challenge • T (page 135)

1. Tempestuous
2. Transient
3. Turbulent
4. Tolerate
5. Turmoil
6. Thesis
7. Trident
8. Transept
9. Tantalize
10. Troglodyte
11. Tentative
12. Truism
13. Taxidermy
14. Trousseau
15. Travesty
16. Tranquil
17. Tarpaulin
18. Tonsorial
19. Tirade
20. Trajectory
21. Thrifty
22. Territory
23. Tepid
24. Tenacious

# - DAY TWENTY-ONE -

## Complete the Word Challenge • U-W (page 137)

| | | |
|---|---|---|
| 1. Vivacious | 9. Urbane | 17. Vigilance |
| 2. Undulation | 10. Vermilion | 18. Vestibule |
| 3. Utility | 11. Whimper | 19. Vernacular |
| 4. Vacation | 12. Vagabond | 20. Wilderness |
| 5. Vertigo | 13. Vociferous | 21. Winsome |
| 6. Valor | 14. Unanimous | 22. Vindictive |
| 7. Vulnerable | 15. Venerate | 23. Wizened |
| 8. Vanquish | 16. Writhe | 24. Valuation |

## Four-Letter Words (page 138)

1. an access or entrance, especially to a mine
2. eager, expectant, on the move
3. greedy, eager
4. uneven, crooked, askew
5. to portend, promise well or ill
6. to give up, grant, surrender
7. state of unnatural, heavy sleep
8. a difficult matter or puzzle
9. wet, exceedingly damp
10. skilful, dextrous, neat
11. the substance of a matter, the essence
12. ready, fluent, easy
13. an indication, suggestion
14. an image or statue
15. species of tree including the holly
16. the Greek Letter I, also a small particle or atom
17. side post of a doorway, window etc, or projecting part of a wall
18. a twist in a rope or wire, a mental twist
19. a stringed musical instrument

20. a person's manner or bearing
21. swamp, bog, mud, dirt
22. hop-drying kiln
23. common, numerous, widespread
24. a large, heavy book

## Latin Phrases (page138)

1. in good faith, genuine
2. abbreviation of *ad libitum* - at one's pleasure, as much as one likes
3. indispensable, absolutely necessary
4. without end, for ever
5. dry or firm land, as distinct from the sea or air
6. the existing state of things
7. abbreviation of *pro tempore* - for the time being, temporarily
8. ("it does not follow") - a conclusion which does not follow from the premises
9. time flies
10. proportionally, in proportion to the value of
11. one thing in place of or in return for another, tit for tat
12. as a whole, completely
13. of last month
14. by the year, yearly
15. with stronger reason
16. let the buyer beware
17. beneath one's dignity
18. by that very fact, by the fact itself
19. beyond the powers or legal authority of
20. in reverse, conversely
21. under consideration of a court or judge
22. in secret, in a closed court
23. by or in itself, intrinsically
24. in discharge of duty, in virtue of one's office

## TWO EXTRA QUIZZES!
### Strange Words • 2 (page 159)

37. a sponge or brush made of plant-fiber
38. a vegetable, a variety of beet
39. to puzzle or mystify, to puzzle out
40. a half, one of two parts
41. to coddle a person; one who is coddled or nursed
42. a state of depression, stomach-ache
43. an object of senseless veneration
44. feeby sentimental, insipidly pretty
45. mincing, affected, lacking in spirit
46. a fool, blockhead or simpleton
47. abuse, detraction, evil-speaking, being ill-spoken of
48. the number eight, or a set or group of eight
49. a furniture warehouse, a furniture-removing van
50. a trifling offence or fault
51. chicanery, petty quibbling
52. a rogue, thief, pirate
53. a paltry poet
54. an inquisitive person, gossip, newsmonger
55. a ragged, dirty fellow
56. a rascal, rogue ,vagabond
57. boastful talk, extravagant bragging
58. a quarrel, muddle or melee
59. to vacillate, be irresolute or undecided
60. a slobbering or dirty fellow
61. a metrical foot of two long syllables
62. to fasten or stretch out like a spread eagle, to beat completely
63. a long-handled implement for removing water
64. a small fish
65. conjunction or opposition (in astronomy)
66. a ragged or beggarly fellow
67. chatter, prattle, gossip

68. upside down, disorderly
69. a tuft or clump of grass
70. a book or thing carried about on the person
71. printers' annual outing or festivity
72. a newly-weaned child or animal

**Last Words (page 160)**

1. blue pigment or dye, the color of the sky
2. relating to Byzantium or its architecture
3. a Bohemian, a native of Czechoslovakia
4. suffering from dyspepsia or indigestion
5. the nest of a bird of prey, especially an eagle
6. not firm or sound, spongy, blurred, fluffy
7. shackle or fetter
8. affected by hysteria, morbidly excited
9. a climbing evergreen shrub
10. the placing of two or more things close together
11. a strait or narrow channel between two islands
12. a player on the lyre, a lyric poet
13. a disease of rabbits
14. morbid sexual desire in females
15. an instrument for measuring the ozone in the air
16. the vessel in which consecrated bread is kept
17. the result obtained by dividing one number by another
18. a species of cereal plant
19. without system
20. native of ancient Tyre
21. resembling a vulture, ravenous
22. a legendary animal in the form of a winged dragon
23. a musical instrument
24. Christmas and its festivities

**That's It! Hope you enjoyed the book!**

# TWO EXTRA QUIZZES

## STRANGE WORDS • 2

There are some very strange words in the English language. Here are a few of them, some familiar and some not so familiar. How many do you know the meaning of?

37. Loofah

38. Mangelwurzel

39. Metagrobolize

40. Moiety

41. Molly-coddle

42. Mulligrubs

43. Mumbo Jumbo

44. Namby-pamby

45. Niminy-piminy

46. Nincompoop

47. Obloquy

48. Ogdoad

49. Pantechnicon

50. Peccadillo

51. Pettifogging

52. Picaroon

53. Poetaster

54. Quidnunc

55. Ragamuffin

56. Rapscallion

57. Rodomontade

58. Shemozzle

59. Shilly-shally

60. Slubberdegullion

61. Spondee

62. Spread-eagle

63. Squeegee

64. Stickleback

65. Syzygy

66. Tatterdemalion

67. Tittle-tattle

68. Topsy-turvy

69. Tussock

70. Vade-mecum

71. Wayzgoose

72. Weanling

## LAST WORDS

In this final quiz, there is one last common word under each letter. Provide their definitions.

1. Azure
2. Byzantine
3. Czech
4. Dyspeptic
5. Eyrie
6. Fuzzy
7. Gyve
8. Hysterical
9. Ivy
10. Juxtaposition
11. Kyle
12. Lyrist
13. Myxomatosis
14. Nymphomania
15. Ozonoscope
16. Pyx
17. Quotient
18. Rye
19. Systemless
20. Tyrian
21. Vulturous
22. Wyvern
23. Xylophone
24. Yule